Very Short Answers to Very Big Questions
from Very Short Introductions

VERY SHORT INTRODUCTIONS are for anyone wanting a stimulating and accessible way in to a new subject. They are written by experts, and have been published in more than 25 languages worldwide.

The series began in 1995, and now represents a wide variety of topics in history, philosophy, religion, science, and the humanities. Over the next few years it will grow to a library of around 200 volumes – a Very Short Introduction to everything from ancient Egypt and Indian philosophy to conceptual art and cosmology.

Very Short Introductions available now:

AFRICAN HISTORY
John Parker and Richard Rathbone
AMERICAN POLITICAL PARTIES
AND ELECTIONS L. Sandy Maisel
THE AMERICAN PRESIDENCY
Charles O. Jones
ANARCHISM Colin Ward
ANCIENT EGYPT Ian Shaw
ANCIENT PHILOSOPHY Julia Annas
ANCIENT WARFARE
Harry Sidebottom
ANGLICANISM Mark Chapman
THE ANGLO-SAXON AGE John Blair
ANIMAL RIGHTS David DeGrazia
ANTISEMITISM Steven Beller
ARCHAEOLOGY Paul Bahn
ARCHITECTURE Andrew Ballantyne
ARISTOTLE Jonathan Barnes
ART HISTORY Dana Arnold
ART THEORY Cynthia Freeland
THE HISTORY OF ASTRONOMY
Michael Hoskin
ATHEISM Julian Baggini
AUGUSTINE Henry Chadwick
AUTISM Uta Frith
BARTHES Jonathan Culler
BESTSELLERS John Sutherland
THE BIBLE John Riches
THE BRAIN Michael O'Shea
BRITISH POLITICS Anthony Wright
BUDDHA Michael Carrithers
BUDDHISM Damien Keown
BUDDHIST ETHICS Damien Keown
CAPITALISM James Fulcher
CATHOLICISM Gerald O'Collins
THE CELTS Barry Cunliffe
CHAOS Leonard Smith

CHOICE THEORY Michael Allingham
CHRISTIAN ART Beth Williamson
CHRISTIANITY Linda Woodhead
CITIZENSHIP Richard Bellamy
CLASSICS Mary Beard and
John Henderson
CLASSICAL MYTHOLOGY
Helen Morales
CLAUSEWITZ Michael Howard
THE COLD WAR Robert McMahon
CONSCIOUSNESS Susan Blackmore
CONTEMPORARY ART
Julian Stallabrass
CONTINENTAL PHILOSOPHY
Simon Critchley
COSMOLOGY Peter Coles
THE CRUSADES Christopher Tyerman
CRYPTOGRAPHY
Fred Piper and Sean Murphy
DADA AND SURREALISM
David Hopkins
DARWIN Jonathan Howard
THE DEAD SEA SCROLLS
Timothy Lim
DEMOCRACY Bernard Crick
DESCARTES Tom Sorell
DESIGN John Heskett
DINOSAURS David Norman
DOCUMENTARY FILM
Patricia Aufderheide
DREAMING J. Allan Hobson
DRUGS Leslie Iversen
THE EARTH Martin Redfern
ECONOMICS Partha Dasgupta
EGYPTIAN MYTH Geraldine Pinch
EIGHTEENTH-CENTURY BRITAIN
Paul Langford

PAUL E. P. Sanders
PHILOSOPHY Edward Craig
PHILOSOPHY OF LAW
    Raymond Wacks
PHILOSOPHY OF SCIENCE
    Samir Okasha
PHOTOGRAPHY Steve Edwards
PLATO Julia Annas
POLITICAL PHILOSOPHY
    David Miller
POLITICS Kenneth Minogue
POSTCOLONIALISM Robert Young
POSTMODERNISM Christopher Butler
POSTSTRUCTURALISM
    Catherine Belsey
PREHISTORY Chris Gosden
PRESOCRATIC PHILOSOPHY
    Catherine Osborne
PSYCHIATRY Tom Burns
PSYCHOLOGY
    Gillian Butler and Freda McManus
THE QUAKERS Pink Dandelion
QUANTUM THEORY
    John Polkinghorne
RACISM Ali Rattansi
RELATIVITY Russell Stannard
RELIGION IN AMERICA Timothy Beal
THE RENAISSANCE Jerry Brotton
RENAISSANCE ART
    Geraldine A. Johnson
ROMAN BRITAIN Peter Salway
THE ROMAN EMPIRE
    Christopher Kelly
ROUSSEAU Robert Wokler
RUSSELL A. C. Grayling
RUSSIAN LITERATURE Catriona Kelly
THE RUSSIAN REVOLUTION
    S. A. Smith

SCHIZOPHRENIA
    Chris Frith and Eve Johnstone
SCHOPENHAUER
    Christopher Janaway
SCIENCE AND RELIGION
    Thomas Dixon
SCOTLAND Rab Houston
SEXUALITY Véronique Mottier
SHAKESPEARE Germaine Greer
SIKHISM Eleanor Nesbitt
SOCIAL AND CULTURAL
    ANTHROPOLOGY
    John Monaghan and Peter Just
SOCIALISM Michael Newman
SOCIOLOGY Steve Bruce
SOCRATES C. C. W. Taylor
THE SPANISH CIVIL WAR
    Helen Graham
SPINOZA Roger Scruton
STATISTICS David Hand
STUART BRITAIN John Morrill
TERRORISM Charles Townshend
THEOLOGY David F. Ford
THE HISTORY OF TIME
    Leofranc Holford-Strevens
TRAGEDY Adrian Poole
THE TUDORS John Guy
TWENTIETH-CENTURY BRITAIN
    Kenneth O. Morgan
THE UNITED NATIONS
    Jussi M. Hanhimäki
THE VIETNAM WAR
    Mark Atwood Lawrence
THE VIKINGS Julian Richards
WITTGENSTEIN A. C. Grayling
WORLD MUSIC Philip Bohlman
THE WORLD TRADE
    ORGANIZATION Amrita Narlikar

Available Soon:

APOCRYPHAL GOSPELS Paul Foster
EXPRESSIONISM Katerina Reed-Tsocha
FREE SPEECH Nigel Warburton
MODERN JAPAN
    Christopher Goto-Jones

NOTHING Frank Close
PHILOSOPHY OF RELIGION
    Jack Copeland and Diane Proudfoot
SUPERCONDUCTIVITY
    Stephen Blundell

For more information visit our websites
www.oup.com/uk/vsi
www.oup.com/us

VERY SHORT ANSWERS TO VERY BIG QUESTIONS

from Very Short Introductions

OXFORD
UNIVERSITY PRESS

OXFORD
UNIVERSITY PRESS

Great Clarendon Street, Oxford OX2 6DP

Oxford University Press is a department of the University of Oxford.
It furthers the University's objective of excellence in research, scholarship,
and education by publishing worldwide in

Oxford New York

Auckland Cape Town Dar es Salaam Hong Kong Karachi
Kuala Lumpur Madrid Melbourne Mexico City Nairobi
New Delhi Shanghai Taipei Toronto

With offices in

Argentina Austria Brazil Chile Czech Republic France Greece
Guatemala Hungary Italy Japan Poland Portugal Singapore
South Korea Switzerland Thailand Turkey Ukraine Vietnam

Oxford is a registered trade mark of Oxford University Press
in the UK and in certain other countries

Published in the United States
by Oxford University Press Inc., New York

British Library Cataloguing in Publication Data

Data available

Library of Congress Cataloging in Publication Data

Data available

ISBN 978-0-19-956358-6

1 3 5 7 9 10 8 6 4 2

Typeset by SPI Publisher Services, Pondicherry, India
Printed in Great Britain by
Clays Ltd., St Ives plc

Contents

List of illustrations

Introduction

As we draw near to the end of the first decade of the 21st century, what are the BIG questions?

Some have been puzzling humankind since it first learned to think and believe. Can life without a creator have any meaning? Will the world expire, and if so, when and how?

Others need to be solved *now*. Are there any quick fixes for the looming catastrophe of global warming? What can we do about the AIDS pandemic? Is helping someone to die a humane act or murder? Are nuclear weapons the ultimate sanction or the terrorist's new weapon of choice?

A few may astonish us. Sex is surely an immutable part of human existence, but it too is progressing in astonishing ways: what is the future of sex? As intelligence test scores increase generation after generation: how much cleverer will our grandchildren be than ourselves? And when will the first robot with feelings be created (because it's not a question of 'whether' anymore!)?

Very Short Introductions tackle the subjects we all need to know about – in history, politics, faith, philosophy, science, society, the arts and culture ... But these books don't just assemble *facts*. They present invigorating and thought-provoking analysis of each subject. And they never shy away from difficult questions, presenting both sides of arguments that can often be clouded by insufficient grasp of the facts or muddled thinking. Does immigration benefit the host population? Is our right to privacy absolute? *Very Short Introductions* provides answers with reference to the latest research and expert thinking.

Here readers will experience some of the exciting questions answered by sixteen books in the series. But *Very Short Introductions* offer the chance to master more than 200 subjects from *Ancient History* to *The Meaning of Life*, and in doing so, to discover answers to many more vital questions. What actually is 'race'? – in *Racism*. Where is the threshold between coercive interrogation and torture? – in *Human Rights*. And in the year when citizens of the globe's greatest superpower go to the polls to elect arguably the world's most powerful leader: why do relatively few Americans vote? – in *American Political Parties and Elections*.

Very Short Introductions can't answer all of life's big questions, but they will equip anyone who cares to address them with an understanding of what is involved, and how, one day, they may be solved.

Chapter 1
Is it possible to build a robot with feelings?

The following text is extracted from *Emotion: A Very Short Introduction* by Dylan Evans

Giving computers emotions could be very useful for a whole variety of reasons. For a start, it would be much easier and more enjoyable to interact with an emotional computer than with today's unemotional machines. Imagine if your computer could recognize what emotional state you were in each time you sat down to use it, perhaps by scanning your facial expression. You arrive at work one Monday morning, and the computer detects that you are in a bad mood. Rather than simply asking you for your password, as computers do today, the emotionally aware desktop PC might tell you a joke, or suggest that you read a particularly nice e-mail first. Perhaps it has learnt from previous such mornings that you resent such attempts to cheer you up. In this case, it might ignore you until you had calmed down or had a coffee. It might be much more productive to work with a computer that was emotionally intelligent in this way than with today's dumb machines.

This is not just a flight of fancy. Computers are already capable of recognizing some emotions. Ifran Essa and Alex Pentland, two American computer scientists, have designed a program that enables a computer to recognize facial expressions of six basic emotions. When volunteers pretended to feel one of these emotions, the computer recognized the emotion correctly

98 per cent of the time. This is even better than the accuracy rate achieved by most humans on the same task. If computers are already better than us at recognizing some emotions, it is surely not long before they will acquire similarly advanced capacities for expressing emotions, and perhaps even for feeling them. In the future, it may be humans who are seen by computers as emotionally illiterate, not vice versa.

What other applications might there be for emotional computers besides providing emotionally intelligent interfaces for desktop PCs? Rosalind Picard, a computer scientist at the MIT Media Laboratory in Boston, has proposed dozens of possible uses, including the following:

- artificial interviewers that train you how to do well in job interviews by giving you feedback on your body language;
- affective voice synthesizers that allow people with speech problems not just to speak, but to speak in genuinely emotional ways;
- frustration monitors that allow manufacturers to evaluate how easy their products are to use;
- wearable computers ('intelligent clothing') that give you feedback on your emotional state, so that you can tell when you are getting stressed and need a break.

All of these applications involve giving computers the ability to recognize what emotions a human is feeling, and to respond appropriately. But what about giving computers the ability to feel emotions themselves? What possible use could this be?

Mr Spock of Star Trek fame, could never have evolved. A creature without emotions could not survive in a dangerous and unpredictable world like ours. Emotions are not luxuries. Still less are they obstacles to intelligent action. They are vital to the survival of any reasonably complex creature.

The same point applies to mobile robots. A robot that is not confined to the safe environment of the laboratory will sooner or later be confronted by dangers such as moving objects or deep holes. If the robot is being directed by a human via remote control, the human can steer the robot around or away from such obstacles. But it is not always desirable to make the robot so dependent on a human driver. Nor is it always possible. When the spacecraft Deep Space 1 flew past the asteroid Braille in July 1999, it was too far away from earth for ground control to direct all its movements. The radio waves took too long to travel from earth to the spacecraft, so split-second decisions had to be taken by the spacecraft itself, using its on-board autonomous navigation ('auto-nav') software to plot its own course. It even made its own decisions about when to take photographs.

NASA wants more of this 'hands-off' technology, because it frees up the expensive and overbooked Deep Space Network of large radio antennae for more interesting things than routine tracking of spacecraft. It also allows unmanned spacecraft to handle unpredicted events in real time, without waiting for ground control to tell them what to do. Since most spacecraft like Deep Space 1 usually fly at speeds over 50,000 km per hour, this time saving could be vital.

Auto-nav software is just the beginning. Intelligent machines that can make their own decisions and cope with unpredictability will be useful in many other areas beyond spaceflight. They might be used in bomb disposal, micro-surgery, search-and-rescue missions, and espionage. In all these situations, a robot without the capacity to detect dangers and respond accordingly – without *fear*, that is – would not last very long. A robot with several potentially conflicting goals, such as avoiding obstacles, refuelling, taking photographs, and returning to earth as fast as possible, will need some kind of internal goal management system. The problem of managing conflicting goals is known by computer scientists as 'the robot's dilemma'. Way back in 1967, Herbert Simon – one of the pioneers of artificial intelligence – argued that robots would need emotions to solve this dilemma.

Simon's argument was simple but clever. There is a limit to the amount of things that any agent can do at any one time, whether it be an animal or a robot. Therefore, if the agent has more than one goal, it must divide its time up wisely, allotting the right amount to each activity in pursuit of each goal. However, unless the environment is completely stable and benign, the agent must also remain alert to external changes that may require a rapid change of activity. Suppose, for example, that a robot has the following two goals: *first* to collect rock samples from an asteroid and analyse them *in situ*, and, *secondly*, to bring these samples safely back to earth. Now imagine that such a robot is sitting happily on the asteroid, conducting some chemical test on the rock it has just picked up, when suddenly a piece of debris comes hurtling towards it. Unless the robot has some kind of 'interruption mechanism', it may succeed in its first goal, but fail dismally in the second.

Simon proposed that emotions were just such interruption mechanisms. He meant this as a definition. In other words, the word 'emotion' is the name we have given to these interruption mechanisms when we have observed them in ourselves and other animals. This is not a neurobiological *or* a behavioural definition of emotion, but a functional one. Functional definitions are like behavioural definitions in that they define mental processes by reference to observable actions, but, unlike full-blooded behaviourists, functionalists do not require that these actions actually take place for the process to be said to occur. It is enough to say that the action would have resulted if certain other mental processes had been in place too. According to Simon's functional definition, emotions are those mental processes that generally work to interrupt activity in rapid response to a sudden environmental change.

The keyword in this definition is *rapid*. Lots of mental processes can interrupt other processes, but not all do so in rapid response to a sudden change in the environment. A mood may build up gradually in response to many small changes before it is sufficiently powerful to interrupt our thoughts. By identifying emotions with *rapid-response* interruption mechanisms, Simon may have been too narrow. His definition works well for basic emotions, which are typically of rapid onset, but it fares less well for higher cognitive emotions such as love or envy, which may build up more slowly – usually longer than a few seconds, at least. Like many good definitions, Simon's definition of emotion has its value in highlighting one important feature, but it does not cover all cases.

What if machines evolve emotions on their own?

All of the potential applications for emotional machines discussed so far have been resolutely utilitarian. This is all very well, but I think that most emotional machines in the future will be built not for any practical purpose, but purely for entertainment. If you want to envision the future of affective computing, do not think spacecraft and intelligent clothing – think toys and video games.

Many video games already use simple learning algorithms to control non-player characters, such as monsters and baddies. In *Tomb Raider*, for example, the enemies faced by Lara Croft need only a few shots before they cotton on to your shooting style. If you are lying in wait for a dinosaur, it might remain in the shadows, tempting you to come out and take a pot shot so that it can attack you more easily. These are relatively simple programs, but the constant demand for better games means that the software is continually improving. It might well be that the first genuinely emotional computers are games consoles rather than spacecraft.

Other entertainment software with proto-emotional capacities is also available in the form of the virtual pets who live in personal computers. Many kids now keep dogs and cats as screen pets, and more recently a virtual baby has been launched. A program called the Sims lets you design your own people, but they soon take on a life of their own, which can be fascinating to watch. The Sims are eerily human in their range of emotional behaviour. They get angry, become depressed, and even fall in love.

All these creatures are virtual – they live inside your computer, and their only 'body' is a picture on a screen. However, the first computerized creatures with real bodies are also now coming onto the toy market, and they too have proto-emotional capacities. First came little furry robots called 'Furbies', which fall asleep when tired, and make plaintiff cries when neglected for too long. Now there are also robotic dogs and cats that run around your living room without ever making a mess.

As with Kismet, people respond to these artificial life forms with natural sympathy. Their minds are not filled with ponderous doubts about whether these emotions are 'real' or not. They simply enjoy playing with them, as they would with a real kitten or baby. There is even a baby doll with a silicon brain and a latex face that screws up into an expression of distress when it needs feeding.

The gap between science fiction and science fact is closing. Today's computers and robots still have a long way to go before they acquire HAL's emotional repertoire, but they have already made some progress. In fact, the technology is advancing so quickly that some people are already worried about what will happen when computers and robots become as emotional as we are. Will they turn against their creators, like HAL? In the film *Terminator*, a giant computer called Skynet becomes self-aware and attempts to prevent humans from turning it off by tapping into the military's command system and launching its nuclear missiles. Will affective computing lead ultimately to a battle between humans and machines? If so, who will win? Perhaps in the future robots will no longer be our toys – we may be theirs.

We might be able to avoid this grim fate by programming computers to be subservient to us. We might, for example, program them to follow the 'the three laws of robotics', as Isaac Asimov suggested in his short story, 'The Bicentennial Man', which was the inspiration for the film of the same name (see Box below).

However, an important aspect of many emotions is that they are unpredictable. A genuinely emotional robot might decide not to obey these laws, or reinterpret them. And, just as there is a growing respect for animal rights these days, based at least in part on the recognition that non-human animals feel pain and emotions just like human animals, so we might foresee a growing respect for robot rights, based on similar grounds. Just as some people are prepared to use violent means to defend animal rights, so some people might join forces with the oppressed robots to free them from their slavery.

Many people might think that computers will always be predictable, since all they ever do is follow a program. The same idea leads people to reject the idea that computers might one day come to have emotions. Even if we design clever software that allows a computer to mimic emotional behaviour, these will not be true emotions, because they will just be following instructions.

The three laws of robotics

1. A robot may not injure a human being or, through inaction, allow a human being to come to harm.

2. A robot must obey the orders given it by human beings except where such orders would conflict with the First Law.

3. A robot must protect its own existence as long as such protection does not conflict with the First or Second Law.

Source: Isaac Asimov, 'The Bicentennial Man'

The computer would not be unpredictable, as genuinely emotional creatures are.

What, then, would these people say of computers that evolve their own programs? Such machines might come to have true emotions of their own, not designed by any human. A relatively recent branch of computer science, known as artificial life, experiments with just such self-evolving software. Instead of writing the program themselves, computer scientists working in artificial life generate random sequences of instructions, and allow these mini-programs (called genetic algorithms) to compete with each other for space on the computer's hard disk. The programs that perform better than others in the task at hand are allowed to make copies of themselves and occupy more memory space, while those that perform badly are erased. The copying process, however, is deliberately made imperfect, so that the occasional error creeps in. This provides for the generation of mutant programs, some of which are even better at performing the chosen task than their parents and so come to dominate the hard disk. If this process is repeated for many generations, the beneficial mutations accumulate, leading to exceptionally effective programs that no human could have designed by normal methods.

It will not have escaped your notice that artificial life is remarkably like evolution by natural selection. In fact, it *is* evolution by natural selection. All the ingredients are there: heredity (they make copies of themselves), mutation (the copies are not perfect), and differential replication (some programs make more copies of themselves than others). The technical term for these self-evolving programs – 'genetic algorithms' – makes clear the parallel with DNA-based evolution. The fact that the protagonists are sequences of code on a hard disk rather than sequences of nucleotides on a chromosome does not disqualify artificial life from evolution. Just as it would be parochial to deny that computers could not have emotions because they lack organic brains, so it would be equally parochial to deny that they could evolve simply because they lack DNA. The essence of all biological processes, from emotion and evolution to life itself, lies not in the materials of which they are composed but in how those materials behave. So long as programs can make copies of themselves, some of which are not perfect, and so long as the number of copies made depends on some property of the program itself, the programs can truly be said to evolve by natural selection.

One of the most famous experiments in artificial life involved the creation of a virtual world known as *Tierra*. Designed by the computer scientist Thomas Ray, *Tierra* was initially populated with copies of a single program. As just described, this program had the ability to make copies of itself; it was a 'genetic algorithm'. But the copies were not always perfect, so, as time went on, *Tierra* became filled with an increasingly diverse population of digital organisms. As Ray observed the evolution of his virtual biosphere, he was fascinated to see the emergence of unforeseen life forms, complete with virtual viruses and hosts who developed artificial immune systems to defend themselves. These artificial life forms did not get as far as acquiring emotions, but it is not hard to see how they could come to evolve such capacities, if they were given enough time. Given the random element in the design process, such artificial emotions could be genuinely unpredictable.

The techniques of artificial life may be enough to persuade those who reject the possibility of emotional machines on the grounds that true emotions are unpredictable. Such techniques, however, will probably not be enough to meet the last and most pressing objection to the idea of affective computers. This is the contention that computers will never have true emotions because they will never be conscious. According to this view, computers might come to exhibit emotional *behaviour*, but they will never have that subjective *feeling* that constitutes the essence of true emotion.

11

As already noted, many people seem to regard feelings as the essence of emotion, but this is not the view taken by most contemporary scientists and philosophers who study emotion. From the viewpoint of modern science, it would be as foolish to deny that a computer could have emotions just because it lacked conscious feelings as to deny that a paralysed person could have emotions simply because he could not make the relevant facial expressions.

Furthermore, the claim that computers could never become conscious is just an intuition. Some rather specious arguments have been put forward to support this intuition, but these thought experiments, involving Chinese rooms and zombies, are even more far-fetched than the idea they oppose. The truth is that, at the beginning of the twenty-first century, no one really has much of an idea about what consciousness really is. Given the lack of good ideas about consciousness, and the lack of agreement about how to investigate it, all objections against emotional computing based on the supposed impossibility of conscious machines must be taken with a pinch of salt.

One of the few good ideas about consciousness that has gained some measure of agreement is that subjective feelings depend very much on the kind of body you have. This might mean that the digital organisms in *Tierra* could never become conscious, as they are merely virtual. They exist only as sequences of code on a computer's hard disk. More recently, however, computer scientists have begun to extend the techniques of artificial life to computers with real bodies. This fledgling discipline is known as evolutionary robotics. As with artificial life, the idea is to let the program that controls the robot evolve by itself, rather than getting humans to design it. Even if the Tierran organisms could not become conscious, such embodied programs might be able to.

If emotions are vital to the survival of any half-intelligent creature, we should expect these complex robots to evolve their own

Will computers ever become conscious?

Some researchers in artificial intelligence think that machines will become conscious within the next hundred years. Some philosophers think this is ridiculous. They claim that machines could *never* become conscious, and they have devised some curious thought-experiments to support this claim.

In what has now become a classic paper in the philosophy of mind, John Searle proposed the idea of the 'Chinese room'. A man sits in a room into which are fed a series of Chinese inscriptions. He is armed with a set of rules about how to respond to these inscriptions, which he duly carries out. The people outside the room might think that the man knows Chinese, but it is clear to us that he doesn't. He is only following rules. Searle thinks computers will always be like this. They can only follow rules, but never really 'know' anything. By extension, Searle argues that computers could never become conscious.

Another philosopher, David Chalmers, has argued that consciousness is not something that could ever be demonstrated by behaviour alone. He asks us to imagine a zombie, by which he means a being like us in every external way but without consciousness. If such a being were possible, it would show that we cannot definitely attribute consciousness to a computer no matter how conscious it *seems*.

The problem with these thought-experiments is that, to borrow a phrase, there is too much thought and not enough experiment. Rather than trying to decide whether or not computers can become conscious on the basis of far-fetched stories about other things that we are even less sure about,

> like Chinese rooms and zombies, we would be better off
> proceeding more experimentally. In short, the only way we
> will really know whether or not machines can be conscious is
> by trying to build a conscious machine.

emotions just as the higher animals have done. Left to their own devices, such robots might come to evolve emotions very different from our own. The emotions that a creature needs to survive depend very much on the creature's lifestyle and habitat. If the creature lives a largely solitary existence, it will not need social emotions such as guilt and jealousy. If there are no predators to prey on it, it may not need the capacity to feel afraid. Depending on how different the lifestyle and habitat of robots are from our own, they may come to evolve rather alien kinds of emotion.

Even if robot emotions turn out to be superficially identical to human emotions, they may *feel* very different to the robots themselves. If there really is a close link between consciousness and the details of the body, the subjective feel of our emotions may be determined by the precise details of our physiology. Emotional robots with plastic or metal bodies would then almost certainly have rather different inner sensations from emotional humans with fleshy bodies. Given that sympathy involves taking on the emotions of another and feeling them as if they were one's own, the different physiologies of robots and humans might make it very hard for us to sympathize with them, even if they displayed very human-like behaviour. More dangerously, perhaps, it might be equally difficult for robots to sympathize with us. Once again, the nightmare scenario of a war between humans and robots seems to loom.

Perhaps our fears of a future battle for supremacy between man and machine are misplaced. Complex robots that evolve their own emotions might come to be our friends rather than our enemies.

Bicentennial Man and *Blade Runner* both show humans and robots falling in love with each other.

Such images of friendly robots are even more common in Japan than in the West. The emotional machines that will almost certainly exist in the not too far distant future may even turn out to be our salvation, guiding us out of our hostility towards them by educating us to emulate their own, much more refined sensibility.

Chapter 2
How modern is China?

The following text is extracted from *Modern China: A Very Short Introduction* by Rana Mitter

China is a profoundly modern society; but the way in which its modernity has been manifested is indelibly shaped by the legacy of its premodern (a term preferable to 'traditional') past. Not that the premodern past was ever monolithic or static: China changed immeasurably over hundreds of years, developing a bureaucracy, science, and technology (the invention of gunpowder, clocks, and the compass), a highly commercialized economy (from around 1000 onwards), and a diverse syncretic religious culture.

The similarity in many developments in Europe and China in the period 1000 to around 1800 should not, however, conceal the fact that imperial China and early modern Europe also *differed* widely in their assumptions and mindsets. The development of modernity in the Western world was underpinned by a set of assertions, many of which are still powerful today, about the organization of society. Most central was the idea of 'progress' as the driving force in human affairs. Philosophers such as Descartes and Hegel ascribed to modernity a rationality and teleology, an overarching narrative, that suggested that the world was moving in a particular direction – and that that direction, overall, was a positive one. There were several drivers of progress. One was the idea that dynamic change was a good thing in its own right: in premodern societies, the force of change was often feared as destructive, but the modern mindset welcomed it. In particular, an acceptance and enthusiasm for progress through economic growth, and later, industrial growth, became central to the development of a modern society. Particularly in the formulation of the Enlightenment of the 18th century, the idea of rationality, the ability to make choices and decisions in a predictable, scientific way, also became crucial to the ordering of a modern society.

Modernity also altered the way in which members of society thought of themselves. Society was secularized: modernity was not necessarily hostile to religion, but religion was confined to a defined space within society, rather than penetrating through it. The individual self, able to reason, was now at the centre of the modern world. At the same time, the traditional bonds that the self had to the wider community were broken down; modern societies did not support the old feudal hierarchies of status and bondage, but rather, broke them down in favour of equality, or at any rate, a non-hierarchical model of society.

Above all, societies are modern in large part because they perceive themselves as being so: self-awareness ('enlightenment') is central to modernity and the identities that emerge from it, such as nationhood. This has led the West, in particular, to draw far too strong a distinction between its own 'modern' values and those elsewhere in the world. China, for instance, showed many features over thousands of years that shared assumptions of modernity long before the West had a significant impact there. China used a system of examinations for entry to the bureaucracy from the 10th century CE, a clearly rational and ordered way of trying to choose a power elite, at a time when religious decrees and brute force were doing the same job in much of Europe. At the same time, China started to develop an integrated and powerful commercial economy, with cash crops taking the place of subsistence farming. It is clear that many aspects of 'modernity' were visible earlier and more clearly in China than in Europe.

Among the most powerful elements of modern thought in Europe was its ability to maintain the idea that its own genesis and construction were profoundly different from those of other societies. In part, this was because of a desire to create a profound distinction between Western European politics and that of other societies, particularly in the 19th century, when imperialist ideology became important. Yet in many ways, the attributes of modernity – particularly self-awareness and its associated sense of anti-hierarchy – were drawn from a pre-existing religious tradition, in which birth and rebirth were crucial. While Christianity was clearly one source of this concept (having also provided the cultural grounding for the teleology of progress that underlies classic modernity), the ideas of enlightenment and self-awareness emerged much earlier as part of Buddhist thought, and in later centuries were developed within another path defined by Islam. The most strongly Eurocentric understandings of modernity have found it hard to acknowledge its cross-cultural roots; yet they are there.

But all the same, China before the mid-19th century did not share certain key assumptions of the emerging elites of Europe in the 16th to 19th centuries. China did not, during that time, develop powerful political movements that believed in flattening hierarchies: in the Confucian world, 'all men within the four seas' might be 'brothers', but 'all men' were not equal. Chinese thinkers did not stress the individuated self as a positive good in contrast to the collective, although there was a clear idea of personal development to become a 'gentleman' or 'sage'. Nor, overall, did it make the idea of a teleology of forward progress central to the way it viewed the world: rather, history was an attempt to recapture the lost golden age of the Zhou and ways of the ancients, and rather than praising innovation and dynamic change in its own right, premodern China developed highly sophisticated technology and statecraft while stressing the importance of past precedent, and of order. As for economic growth, while it would be too strong to say that Confucian thought wholly disapproved of trade (the

Ming and Qing saw a comfortable accommodation by the state with the idea of commerce), the concept of economic growth as a good in its own right was not as central to the premodern Chinese mindset as it was to the type of modernity that emerged in Europe.

These assumptions mark a profound difference from China's experience in the contemporary era. Since the early 20th century at least, China's governments and elite thinkers have accepted most of the tenets of modernity, even while vehemently opposing the Western and Japanese imperialism which forced those ideas into China. The Communist and Nationalist governments that dominated China in the 20th century both declared that China was progressing towards the future; that a new, dynamic culture was needed to take it there; that hierarchies needed to be broken down, not preserved; and that while order was important, economic growth was the only way to make China rich and strong. Most notably, China's leaders were much more fiercely and uncompromisingly modern in their assumptions than many of their contemporaries in India or Japan in the early 20th century: the 'May Fourth Movement' of the 1910s was far more eager to reject China's Confucian past completely than figures in India, such as Gandhi, were to reject that society's past.

But at the same time, there is a chimerical element to the quest for modernity. Modernity keeps changing, and Chinese conceptions of it change as well: the modernity of the 'self-strengtheners' who sought to adapt Western technology in the late Qing is not the same as that of the radicals who declared a 'new culture' in the 1910s, nor of the Nationalists and Communists whose primary goal was to find a stable, modern identity for the Chinese state and people. Even today, the question of what a modern China looks like is in flux. At the same time, China's new-found strength means that it is in a much better position than ever before to project aspects of its own model of modernity back into the wider global definition of the term.

With very few exceptions, all of the warring factions that vied over China's future in the 20th century were 'modern', not just in the sense of being 'recent', but in their rejection or adaptation of the Confucian norms of the past, and their embrace of a new set of norms that were derived from outside, but which were adapted to make 'Chinese' and 'modern' compatible, rather than terms which seemed to be in opposition to one another. Although they violated their own rhetoric on countless occasions, China's rulers in the 20th century – and the 21st – have sought to create a nation-state with an equal, self-aware citizen body. This is a profoundly modern goal. But how successful will they be in achieving it.

Chapter 3
What are the science and religion debates really about?

The following text is extracted from *Science and Religion: A Very Short Introduction* by Thomas Dixon

In Rome on 22 June 1633 an elderly man was found guilty by the Catholic Inquisition of rendering himself 'vehemently suspected of heresy, namely, of having held and believed a doctrine which is false and contrary to the divine and Holy Scripture'. The doctrine in question was that 'the sun is the centre of the world and does not move from east to west, that the earth moves and is not the centre of the world, and that one may hold and defend as probable an opinion after it has been declared and defined as contrary to Holy Scripture'. The guilty man was the 70-year-old Florentine philosopher Galileo Galilei, who was sentenced to imprisonment (a punishment that was later commuted to house arrest) and instructed to recite the seven penitential Psalms once a week for the next three years as a 'salutary penance'. That included a weekly recitation of the particularly apt line addressed to God in Psalm 102: 'In the beginning you laid the foundations of the earth, and the heavens are the work of your hands.' Kneeling before the 'Reverend Lord Cardinals, Inquisitors-General', Galileo accepted his sentence, swore complete obedience to the 'Holy Catholic and Apostolic Church', and declared that he cursed and detested the 'errors and heresies' of which he had been suspected – namely belief in a sun-centred cosmos and in the movement of the earth.

It is hardly surprising that this humiliation of the most celebrated scientific thinker of his day by the Catholic Inquisition on the grounds of his beliefs about astronomy and their contradiction of the Bible should have been interpreted by some as evidence of an inevitable conflict between science and religion. The modern encounter between evolutionists and creationists has also seemed to reveal an ongoing antagonism, although this time with science, rather than the church, in the ascendancy. The Victorian agnostic Thomas Huxley expressed this idea vividly in his review of Charles Darwin's *On the Origin of Species* (1859). 'Extinguished theologians,' Huxley wrote, 'lie about the cradle of every science as the strangled snakes beside that of Hercules; and history records that whenever science and orthodoxy have been fairly opposed, the latter has been forced to retire from the lists, bleeding and crushed if not annihilated; scotched, if not slain.' The image of conflict has also been attractive to some religious believers, who use it to portray themselves as members of an embattled but righteous minority struggling heroically to protect their faith against the oppressive and intolerant forces of science and materialism.

Although the idea of warfare between science and religion remains widespread and popular, recent academic writing on the subject has been devoted primarily to undermining the notion of an inevitable conflict. As we shall see, there are good historical reasons for rejecting simple conflict stories. From Galileo's trial in 17th-century Rome to modern American struggles over the latest form of anti-evolutionism, known as 'Intelligent Design', there has been more to the relationship between science and religion than meets the eye, and certainly more than just conflict. Pioneers of early modern science such as Isaac Newton and Robert Boyle saw their work as part of a religious enterprise devoted to understanding God's creation. Galileo too thought that science and religion could exist in mutual harmony. The goal of a constructive and collaborative dialogue between science and religion has been endorsed by many Jews, Christians, and Muslims in the modern world. The idea that scientific and religious views are inevitably in tension is also contradicted by the large numbers of religious scientists who continue to see their research as a complement rather than a challenge to their faith, including the theoretical physicist John Polkinghorne, the former director of the Human Genome Project Francis S. Collins, and the astronomer Owen Gingerich, to name just a few.

Does that mean that conflict needs to be written out of our story altogether? Certainly not. The only thing to avoid is too narrow an idea of the kinds of conflicts one might expect to find between science and religion. The story is not always one of a heroic and open-minded scientist clashing with a reactionary and bigoted church. The bigotry, like the open-mindedness, is shared around on all sides – as are the quest for understanding, the love of truth, the use of rhetoric, and the compromising entanglements with the power of the state. Individuals, ideas, and institutions can and have come into conflict, or been resolved into harmony, in an endless array of different combinations.

The leading historian of science and religion John Hedley Brooke writes that serious historical study has 'revealed so extraordinarily rich and complex a relationship between science and religion in the past that general theses are difficult to sustain. The real lesson turns out to be the complexity.' Some of that historical complexity will be explored in subsequent chapters. There has certainly not been a single and unchanging relationship between two entities called 'science' and 'religion'. There are, nonetheless, some central philosophical and political questions that have frequently recurred in this context: What are the most authoritative sources of knowledge? What is the most fundamental reality? What kind of creatures are human beings? What is the proper relationship between church and state? Who should control education? Can either scripture or nature serve as a reliable ethical guide?

Debates about science and religion are, on the face of it, about the intellectual compatibility or incompatibility of some particular religious belief with some particular aspect of scientific knowledge. Does belief in life after death conflict with the findings of modern brain science? Is belief in the Bible incompatible with believing that humans and chimpanzees evolved from a common ancestor? Does belief in miracles conflict with the strictly law-governed world revealed by the physical sciences? Or can belief in free will and divine action, conversely, be supported and substantiated by the theories of quantum mechanics? One of the answers to the question that is the title of this chapter – What are science–religion debates really about? – is that they are about these issues of intellectual compatibility.

What I especially want to emphasize in this *Very Short Introduction* to the subject, however, is that these contemporary contests of ideas are the visible tips of much larger and deeper-lying structures. My aim throughout this book will be to look historically at how we came to think as we do about science and religion, to explore philosophically what preconceptions about knowledge are involved, and to reflect on the political and ethical questions that often set the unspoken agenda for these intellectual debates. In the rest of this introductory chapter, I indicate the kinds of questions I think we should be asking about science and religion, both as sources of individuals' beliefs and as social and political entities, before also briefly introducing 'science and religion' as an academic field.

Encountering nature

Scientific knowledge is based on observations of the natural world. But observing the natural world is neither as simple nor as solitary an activity as it might sound. Take the moon, for instance. When you look up at the sky on a clear night, what do you see? You see the moon and the stars. But what do you actually observe? There are a lot of small bright lights and then a larger whitish circular object. If you had never learned any science, what would you think this white object was? Is it a flat disc, like a kind of giant aspirin?

Or is it a sphere? If the latter, then why do we always see the same side of it? And why does its shape change from a thin crescent to a full disc and back again? Is it an object like the earth? If so, how big is it? And how close? And do people live there? Or is it a smaller night-time equivalent of the sun? Finally, perhaps it is like one of the little bright lights but larger or closer? In any case, how and why does it move across the sky like that? Is something else pushing it? Is it attached to an invisible mechanism of some kind? Is it a supernatural being?

Now, if you are well informed about modern science, you will know that the moon is a large spherical rocky satellite which orbits the earth completely about once a month and which rotates once on its own axis in the same time (which explains why we always see the same side of it). The changing relative positions of the sun, earth, and moon also explain why the moon displays 'phases' – with either the entirety or only a small crescent of the illuminated half of the moon visible at a particular time. You may also know that all physical bodies are attracted to each other by a gravitational force in proportion to the product of their masses and in inverse proportion to the square of the distance between them, and that this helps to explain the regular motions of the moon around the earth and of the earth around the sun. You will probably also know that the bright little lights in the night sky are stars, similar to our sun; that the ones visible to the naked eye are thousands of light years away and those observable through telescopes are millions or even billions of light years away; so that to look up at the night sky is to look into the distant past of our universe. But however much of all this you know, you did not find it out by observation. You were told it. You possibly learned it from your parents or a science teacher or a television programme or an online encyclopaedia. Even professional astronomers will not generally have checked the truth of any of the statements made in this paragraph by their own empirical observations. The reason for this is not that astronomers are lazy or incompetent, but simply that they can rely on the amassed authoritative observations and theoretical reasonings of the scientific community which, over a period of many centuries, have established these facts as fundamental physical truths.

The point is that while it is certainly true that scientific knowledge is based on and tested against observations of the natural world, there is an awful lot more to it than just pointing your sense organs in the right direction. As an individual, even an individual scientist, only the tiniest fraction of what you know is based directly on your own observations. And even then, those observations only make sense within a complex framework of existing facts and theories which have been accumulated and developed through many centuries. You only know what you do about the moon and the stars because of a long and complex cultural history which mediates between the light from the night sky and your thoughts about astronomy and cosmology. That history includes the successful challenging of the old earth-centred world view by Galileo Galilei, with the help of Copernicus's astronomy and the newly invented telescope in the early 17th century, as well as the establishment of Newton's laws of motion and gravitation later in that century, and more recent developments in physics and cosmology too. It also includes, crucially, the histories of those social and political mechanisms that allow for, and control, the dissemination of scientific knowledge among the people through books and in classrooms.

We should also notice, by the way, that what science often aims to show is that things in themselves are not as they initially seem to us – that appearances can be deceptive. The earth beneath our feet certainly seems to be solid and stable, and the sun and the other stars appear to move around us. But science eventually showed that, despite all the sensory evidence to the contrary, the earth is not only spinning on its own axis but is also hurtling around the sun at great speed. Indeed, one of the characters in Galileo's *Dialogue Concerning the Two Chief World Systems* (1632) expresses his admiration on just these grounds for those who, like

Aristarchus and Copernicus, had been able to believe in the sun-centred system before the advent of the telescope: 'I cannot sufficiently admire the intellectual eminence of those who received it and held it to be true. They have by sheer force of intellect done such violence to their own senses as to prefer what reason told them over that which sense experience plainly showed them to be the case.' In more recent times, both evolutionary biology and quantum mechanics have similarly required people to believe the most implausible things – that we share an ancestor not only with rabbits but also with carrots, for example, or that the smallest components of matter are simultaneously both waves and particles. People sometimes say that science is just a systematization of empirical observations, or nothing more than the careful application of common sense. However, it also has the ambition and the potential to show that our senses deceive us and that our basic intuitions may lead us astray.

But when you look up at the night sky, you may not be thinking about astronomy and cosmology at all. You may instead be gripped by a sense of the power of nature, the beauty and grandeur of the heavens, the vastness of space and time, and your own smallness and insignificance. This might even be a religious experience for you, reinforcing your feeling of awe at the power of God and the immensity and complexity of his creation, putting you in mind of the words of Psalm 19: 'The heavens declare the glory of God; the skies proclaim the work of his hands.'

Such an emotional and religious response to the night sky would, of course, be every bit as historically and culturally mediated as the experience of perceiving the moon and the stars in terms of modern cosmology. Without some kind of religious education you certainly would not be able to quote from the Bible, and you would perhaps not even be able to formulate a developed concept of God. Individual religious experiences, like modern scientific observations, are made possible by long processes of human collaboration in a shared quest for understanding. In the religious case, what intervenes between the light hitting your retina and your thoughts about the glory of God is the lengthy history of a particular sacred text, and its reading and interpretation within a succession of human communities. And, as in the scientific case, one of the lessons learned through that communal endeavour is that things are not as they seem. Religious teachers, as much as scientific ones, try to show their pupils that there is an unseen world behind the observed one – and one which might overturn their most settled intuitions and beliefs.

The political dimension

Among historians of science and religion there have been two interestingly different kinds of attack on the 'conflict narrative' favoured by Enlightenment rationalists, Victorian freethinkers, and modern-day scientific atheists. The first strategy is to replace the overarching image of conflict with that of complexity, and to put emphasis on the very different ways that science–religion interactions have developed at different times, in different places, and in different local circumstances. Some scientists have been religious, others atheists. Some religious denominations welcome modern science, others are suspicious of it. Recognizing that neither 'science' nor 'religion' refers to a simple singular entity is an important part of this approach too, as is acknowledging the existence of considerable national differences. To take just the most obvious example, debates about evolution and religion have, from the beginning of the 20th century and right up to the present day, developed quite differently in the United States than they have in Europe and elsewhere. As I will explain in Chapter 5, the debates about the teaching of evolution in schools that go on in America today emerged through circumstances very specific to that country, most importantly the interpretation of the First Amendment to its Constitution, which prohibits the government from passing any law 'respecting an establishment of religion'.

If this first approach to the conflict narrative is to change the plot, the second involves recasting the leading characters. This approach says: yes, there have been conflicts that seem to be between science and religion, and they are real conflicts, but they are not between science and religion. The question then is: who or what are the real antagonists in this story? In a way, we are then just straight back into the messy details of historical complexity. There is certainly not a simple recasting that works for all cases, but the general idea is that the real conflict is a political one about the production and dissemination of knowledge. The opposition of science versus religion is then seen to be standing proxy for some classic modern political conflicts: the individual versus the state, or secular liberalism versus conservative traditionalism. It is interesting to note that in modern America, for example, campaigners both for and against the teaching of evolution in schools have portrayed themselves as representing the rights and freedoms of the people against an intolerant and authoritarian establishment which is controlling the educational agenda. In the 1920s that establishment was portrayed by defenders of evolution as Christian and conservative, but to some religious groups today it seems that a secular liberal elite have taken control of the education system. Debates about science and religion give certain groups an opportunity to argue their case for greater social influence, and greater control over the mechanisms of state education, a case that rests on quite independent political grounds.

These questions about the politics of knowledge will arise repeatedly in subsequent chapters. For the moment, let us consider just one other example – the philosopher and firebrand Thomas Paine. An unsuccessful corset-maker, sacked tax-collector, and occasional political writer, Paine left his native England to start a new life in America in 1774. On his arrival in Philadelphia, he found work as the editor of the *Pennsylvania Magazine*. A couple of years later, his polemical pamphlet *Common Sense* (1776) was a key factor in persuading the American colonists to go to war against the British government, and established Paine as the bestselling author of the age. An associate of Benjamin Rush, Thomas Jefferson, and others of the founding fathers of the United States of America, Paine's democratic and anti-monarchical political philosophy shaped the Declaration of Independence. After politics, Paine's other great passions were science and engineering. He had attended popular lectures on Newton and astronomy back in England, and he spent many years of his life working on a design for a single-span iron bridge, inspired by the delicacy and strength of one of the great works of nature – the spider's web. His whole philosophy was a scientific one. He saw revolutions in governments paralleling the revolutions of celestial bodies in the heavens. Each was an inevitable, natural, and law-governed process. Later in his life, having had a hand in both the American and French revolutions, he turned his sights from monarchy to Christianity. The institutions of Christianity were as offensive to his enlightened and Newtonian sensibilities as were those of monarchical government. In his *Age of Reason* (1794), Paine complained of 'the continual persecution carried on by the Church, for several hundred years, against the sciences and against the professors of science'.

Paine's version of the conflict narrative makes most sense when seen in its political context. Paine was, indeed, a scientific thinker who was opposed to Christianity. He denounced the Bible, especially the Old Testament, with its stories of 'voluptuous debaucheries' among the Israelites and the 'unrelenting vindictiveness' of their God. To the shock of his friends, Paine wrote of the Bible: 'I sincerely detest it, as I detest everything that is cruel.' Paine also lambasted the 'priestcraft' at work in the 'adulterous' relationship between the Church of England and the British state. What he hoped for, though, was not an end to religion but the replacement of Christian religion by a rational religion based on the study of nature – one which recognized the existence of God, the importance of morality, and the hope for a future life, but did away with scriptures, priests, and the authority of the state. His reasons for this were democratic ones. National churches lorded illegitimate power over the people by claiming special access to divine truths and revelations. But everyone can read the book of nature and understand the goodness, power, and generosity of its author. In the religion of Deism recommended by Paine, there was no need for the people to be in thrall either to priests or to the state. Science could help to replace Christianity by showing that every individual could find God by looking at the night sky rather than by reading the Bible or going to church. 'That which is now called natural philosophy', Paine wrote, 'embracing the whole circle of science of which astronomy occupies the chief place, is the study of the works of God, and of the power and wisdom of God and his works, and is the true theology.'

Paine's democratic ideals, including the separation of church and state, are enshrined in the founding documents of the United States. And in modern America too, it is competing political visions that come into conflict in debates about science and religion. American politicians who deny the truth of the theory of evolution and advocate the teaching of a religiously motivated concept of 'Intelligent Design' in schools do not do so for scientific reasons. They do so, rather, to send a signal – to indicate their general support for Christianity, their opposition to excessively secularist interpretations of the Constitution, and their hostility to naturalistic and materialistic world views.

A final interesting piece of support for the suggestion that what is really at stake in science–religion encounters is politics, is to be found in two mid-20th-century stage plays. Each dramatizes a famous clash between a heroic scientific individual and a reactionary and authoritarian religious establishment, and does so to make primarily political points. Bertolt Brecht's *Life of Galileo* was composed during the 1930s and early 1940s. Brecht was a German communist, opposed to fascism, and living in exile in Denmark and subsequently the United States. The play uses the story of Galileo to investigate the dilemmas faced by a dissident intellectual living under a repressive regime, and also to suggest the importance of pursuing scientific knowledge for moral and social ends rather than purely for its own sake. Brecht saw in the well-known Galileo affair political lessons which could be applied to a world struggling against authoritarian fascism and, in the later version of the play, living in the shadow of the dropping of atomic bombs on Hiroshima and Nagasaki.

Jerome Lawrence and Robert E. Lee's play *Inherit the Wind*, first performed in 1955, and made into a famous film in 1960, was a dramatization of the Scopes 'monkey trial' of 1925. The historical events on which the play was based are discussed in Chapter 5; they centre on the prosecution of a Tennessee school teacher, John Scopes, for teaching evolution in contravention of state law. *Inherit the Wind* used the Scopes case to attack the anti-communist purges of the McCarthy era. Scopes, the heroic evolutionist standing up against a repressive Christian establishment in 1920s Tennessee, stood for the struggle for freedom of opinion, association, and expression by communist sympathizers in the face of a repressive American government machine. Among those sympathizers, incidentally, was Bertolt Brecht, who had been called to testify before the House Committee on Un-American Activities in 1947. In the case both of Brecht's *Galileo* and Lawrence and Lee's *Inherit the Wind*, it was questions of intellectual freedom, political power, and human morality that gave the conflict between science and religion its drama and its interest. The same is true in real life.

Chapter 4
Is euthanasia murder?

The following text is extracted from *Medical Ethics: A Very Short Introduction* by Tony Hope

> Good deeds do not require long statements; but when evil is done
> the whole art of oratory is employed as a screen for it.
>
> (Thucydides)

The practice of euthanasia contradicts one of the oldest and most
venerated of moral injunctions: 'Thou shalt not kill'. The practice
of euthanasia, under some circumstances, is morally required by
the two most widely regarded principles that guide medical
practice: respect for patient autonomy and promoting patient's
best interests. In the Netherlands and Belgium active euthanasia
may be carried out within the law.

In Switzerland and in the US state of Oregon, physician-assisted
suicide, that cousin of euthanasia, is legal if certain conditions are
met. Three times in the last 100 years, the House of Lords in the
UK has given careful consideration to the legalization of
euthanasia, and on each occasion has rejected the possibility.
Throughout the world, societies founded to promote voluntary
euthanasia attract large number of members.

Playing the Nazi card

There is a common, but invalid, argument against euthanasia
that I call 'playing the Nazi card'. This is when the opponent of

euthanasia says to the supporter of euthanasia: 'Your views are just like those of the Nazis'. There is no need for the opponent of euthanasia to spell out the rhetorical conclusion: 'and therefore your views are totally immoral'.

Let me put the argument in a classic form used in philosophy and known as a syllogism (I will say more about syllogisms in Chapter 5):

> Premise 1: Many views held by Nazis are totally immoral.
> Premise 2: Your view (support for euthanasia under some circumstances) is one view held by Nazis.
> Conclusion: Your view is totally immoral.

This is not a valid argument. It would be valid only if all the views held by Nazis were immoral.

I will therefore replace premise 1 by premise 1* as follows:

> Premise 1*: All views held by Nazis are totally immoral.

In this case the argument is *logically* valid, but in order to assess whether the argument is *true* we need to assess the truth of premise 1*.

There are two possible interpretations of premise 1*. One interpretation is a version of the classic false argument known as *argumentum ad hominem* (or *bad company fallacy*): that a particular view is true or false, not because of the reasons in favour or against the view, but by virtue of the fact that a particular person (or group of people) holds that view (see Warburton, 1996). But bad people may hold some good views, and good people may hold some bad views. It is quite possible that a senior Nazi was vegetarian on moral grounds. This fact would be irrelevant to the question of whether there are, or are not, moral grounds in favour of vegetarianism. What is important are the reasons for and against the particular view, not the person who holds it. Hitler's well-known vegetarianism, by the way, was on health, not on moral, grounds (Colin Spencer, 1996).

The other, more promising, interpretation of premise 1* is that those views that are categorized as 'Nazi views' are all immoral. Some particular Nazis may hold some views about some topics that are not immoral, but those would not be 'Nazi views'. The Nazi views being referred to are a set of related views, all immoral, that are driven by racism and involve killing people against their will and against their interests. Thus, when it is said that euthanasia is a Nazi view, what is meant is that it is one of these core immoral views that characterize the immoral Nazi worldview. The problem with this argument, however, is that most supporters of euthanasia – as it is practised in the Netherlands for example – are not supporting the Nazi worldview. Quite the contrary. Those on both sides of the euthanasia debate agree that the Nazi killings that took place under the guise of 'euthanasia' were grossly immoral. The point at issue is whether euthanasia in certain specific circumstances is right or wrong, moral or immoral. All depends on being clear about these specific circumstances and being precise about what is meant by euthanasia. Only then can the arguments for and against legalizing euthanasia be properly evaluated. What is needed is some conceptual clarity.

Patients' best interests

Can it be in someone's best interests to die? I believe it can. The courts believe it can. Most doctors, nurses, and relatives believe it can. The question arises quite frequently in health care. A patient with an incurable and fatal disease may reach a stage where she will die within a day or two, but could be kept alive, with active treatment, for a few weeks more. This situation might occur because the patient gets a chest infection, or because there is a chemical imbalance in her blood, in addition to the underlying fatal disease. Antibiotics, or intravenous fluids, might treat this acute problem although they will do nothing to stop the progress of the underlying disease. All those caring for the patient will often agree that it is in the patient's best interests to die now rather than receive the life-extending treatment. The decision not to treat is even more straightforward if the patient's quality of life is now very poor, perhaps because of sustained and untreatable difficulty in breathing – a distressing feeling that is often more difficult to ameliorate than severe pain. If, however, we thought that it was in the patient's best interests to continue to live, rather than to die within days, we ought to give the life-extending treatment. But we do not think this: we believe it is in her best interests to die now rather than receive the life-extending treatment, because her quality of life, due to the underlying fatal illness, is so poor.

Respecting a patient's wishes

Most countries that put a value on individual liberty allow competent adults to refuse any medical treatment even if such treatment is in the patient's best interests; even if it is life-saving. A Jehovah's Witness, for example, may refuse a life-saving blood transfusion. If doctors were to impose treatment against the will of a competent patient then the doctor would be violating the bodily integrity of the person without consent. In legal terms this would amount to committing a 'battery'.

Passive euthanasia is widely accepted

The withholding, or withdrawing, of treatment is widely accepted as morally right in many circumstances. And it is protected in English law. There are two grounds on which it is accepted:

(1) that it is in the patient's best interests; and
(2) that it is in accord with the patient's wishes.

Either of these two conditions is sufficient reason to support passive euthanasia.

In common with widespread medical practice, I believe that there are circumstances when it is in a person's best interests to die rather than to live. I also believe that a competent person has the right to refuse life-saving treatment. Withholding or withdrawing treatment from a patient is justified in either set of circumstances, even though this will lead to death.

If I am right (and the law in England, the US, Canada, and many other countries supports this position) then why was Dr Cox, a caring English physician, convicted of attempted murder?

What Dr Cox did

Lillian Boyes was a 70-year-old patient with very severe rheumatoid arthritis. The pain seemed to be beyond the reach of painkillers. She was expected to die within a matter of days or weeks. She asked her doctor, Dr Cox, to kill her. Dr Cox injected a lethal dose of potassium chloride for two reasons:

(1) out of compassion for his patient, and
(2) because this is what she wanted him to do.

Dr Cox was charged with, and found guilty of, attempted murder. (The reason for not charging him with murder was that, given her condition, Lillian Boyes could have died from her disease and not from the injection.)

The judge, in directing the jury, said:

Even the prosecution case acknowledged that he [Dr Cox]...was prompted by deep distress at Lillian Boyes' condition; by a belief that she was totally beyond recall and by an intense compassion for her fearful suffering. Nonetheless...if he injected her with potassium chloride for the primary purpose of killing her, or hastening her death, he is guilty of the offence charged [attempted murder]...neither the express wishes of the patient nor of her loving and devoted family can affect the position.

This case clearly established that active (voluntary) euthanasia is illegal (and potentially murder) under English common law. It is noteworthy that the patient was competent and wanted to be killed; close and caring relatives and her doctor (as well as the patient) believed it to be in her best interests to die, and the court did not dispute these facts.

The key difference, on which much legal and moral weight is placed, between the case of Dr Cox and the examples of withholding and withdrawing treatment that are a normal and perfectly legal part of medical practice, is that Dr Cox *killed* Lillian Boyes, and did not simply allow her to die.

Mercy killing

Moral philosophers use 'thought experiments'. These are imaginary and sometimes quite unrealistic situations that tease out and examine the morally relevant features of a situation. They are used to test the consistency of our moral beliefs. The thought experiment that I want you to consider is a case, like the Cox case, of mercy killing.

Mercy killing: the case of the trapped lorry driver

A driver is trapped in a blazing lorry. There is no way in which he can be saved. He will soon burn to death. A friend of the driver is standing by the lorry. This friend has a gun and is a good shot. The driver asks this friend to shoot him dead. It will be less painful for him to be shot than to burn to death.

I want to set aside any legal considerations and ask the purely moral question: should the friend shoot the driver?

There are two compelling reasons for the friend to kill the driver:

1. It will lead to less suffering.
2. It is what the driver wants.

These are the two reasons we have been considering with regard to justifying passive euthanasia. What reasons might you give for believing that the friend should not shoot the driver? I will consider seven reasons.

1. The friend might not kill the driver but might wound him and cause more suffering than if he had not tried to kill him.
2. There may be a chance that the driver will not burn to death but might survive the fire.
3. It is not fair on the friend in the long run: the friend will always bear the guilt of having killed the driver.
4. That although this seems to be a case where it might be right for the friend to kill the driver it would still be wrong to do so; for unless we keep strictly to the rule that killing is wrong, we will slide down a slippery slope. Soon we will be killing people when we mistakenly believe it is in their best interests. And we may slip further and kill people in our interests.
5. The argument from Nature: whereas withholding or withdrawing treatment, in the setting of a dying patient, is allowing nature to take its course, killing is an interference in Nature, and therefore wrong.
6. The argument from Playing God, which is a religious version of the argument from Nature. Killing is 'Playing God' – taking on a role that should be reserved for God alone. Letting die, on the other hand, is not usurping God's role, and may, when done with care and love, be enabling God's will to be fulfilled.

7. Killing is in principle a (great) wrong. The difference between passive euthanasia and mercy killing is that the former involves 'allowing to die' and the latter involves killing; and killing is wrong – it is a fundamental wrong.

How good are these arguments? Let's consider them one by one.

Argument 1

It is true that in real life we cannot be certain of the outcome. If you rely on argument 1 then you are not arguing that mercy killing is wrong in principle, but instead that in the real world we can never be sure that it will end in mercy. I am happy to accept that we can never be absolutely sure that the shooting will kill painlessly. There are three possible types of outcome:

(a) If the friend does not shoot (or if the bullet completely misses) then the driver will die having suffered a considerable amount of pain – let us call this amount X.

(b) The friend shoots and achieves the intended result: that the driver dies almost instantaneously and almost painlessly. In this case the driver will suffer an amount Y where Y is much smaller than X – indeed Y is almost zero if we are measuring suffering from the moment when the friend shoots.

(c) The friend shoots but only wounds the driver, causing him overall an amount of suffering Z, where Z is greater than X.

It is because of possibility (c), according to argument 1, that it would be better that the friend does not shoot the driver.

We can now compare the situation where the friend does not shoot the driver with the situation where the friend does shoot. In the former case the total amount of suffering is X. In the latter case the amount of suffering is either Y (close to zero) or Z (greater than X). Thus, by shooting, the friend may bring about a better state of affairs (less suffering) or a worse state of affairs (more suffering). If what is important is avoiding suffering, then whether it is better to shoot or not depends on the differences between X, Y, and Z and the probabilities of each of these outcomes occurring. If almost instantaneous death is by far the most likely result from shooting, and if the suffering level Z is not a great deal more than X, then it would seem right to shoot the driver because the chances are very much in favour that shooting will lead to significantly less suffering.

We can rarely be completely certain of outcomes. If this uncertainty were a reason not to act we would be completely paralysed in making decisions in life. It would be very unlikely, furthermore, that mercy killing in the medical setting (e.g. what Dr Cox did) would lead to more suffering. I conclude that argument 1 does not provide a convincing argument against voluntary active euthanasia.

Argument 2
Argument 2 is the other side of the coin from argument 1, and suffers the same weakness. The question of whether the chance that the driver might survive outweighs the greater chance that he will suffer greatly, and die, depends on what the probabilities actually are. If it is very unlikely that the driver will survive, then argument 2 is not persuasive.

Supporters of argument 2 might counter this conclusion by arguing that the weight to be given to the remote possibility of rescue from the burning lorry should be infinite. In that case, however low the probability of its occurring, the chance should be taken. There are three responses to this argument: first, what grounds are there for giving infinite weight to the possibility of rescue? Second, if we consider that very remote possibilities of rescue justify not shooting then we could equally well conclude that we should shoot. This is because it is also a remote possibility that the bullet, although intended to kill the driver, might in fact enable him to be rescued (e.g. through blowing open the cab door). Third, if argument 2 provides a convincing reason for rejecting mercy killing, it also provides a convincing reason for rejecting the withholding of medical treatment in all circumstances. This is because giving treatment might provide sufficient extension of life for a 'miracle' to occur and for the person to be cured and live healthily for very much longer.

Argument 3

The third argument fails because it begs the very question that is under debate. The friend should only feel guilt if shooting the driver were the wrong thing to do. But the point at issue is what is the right and wrong thing to do. If it is right to shoot the driver, then the friend should not feel guilty if he shot him (thus reducing the driver's suffering). The possibility of guilt is not a reason, one way or the other, for deciding how the friend should act. Rather we first have to answer the question of what is the right thing to do and only then can we ask whether the friend ought to feel guilty.

Argument 4

Argument 4 is a version of what is known as the 'slippery slope argument'. This is such an important type of argument in medical ethics that I will consider it in more detail in Chapter 5. I will distinguish two types of slippery slope – the logical, or conceptual, slope; and the empirical, or in-practice, slope. The types of reason needed to counter a slippery slope argument depend, as we shall see, on which type of argument is being advanced.

Arguments 5 and 6

The arguments from Nature and from Playing God have, like the slippery slope argument, a more general application in medical ethics. I will consider them in more detail later (Chapter 5).

Argument 7

Of all the arguments considered, it is only argument 7 that views killing as wrong in principle.

Is mercy killing wrong in principle?

At this stage we need to get clear what 'killing' means. Those who believe that mercy killing, but not the common medical practice of passive euthanasia, is wrong in principle do so on the grounds that mercy killing involves *actively* causing death rather than failing to prevent it.

But this is not sufficient. Consider the following medical situation. Morphine is sometimes given to patients close to death from an untreatable illness, in order to ensure that the patient suffers as little pain as possible. In addition to preventing pain, morphine also reduces the depth and frequency of breathing (through its action on the part of the brain that controls respiration). In some situations, although not all, morphine can have the foreseeable effect of shortening the patient's life, as well as reducing pain. A doctor who gave morphine to a terminally ill patient in order to reduce the suffering of the patient and foreseeing (although not intending) the earlier death of the patient, would not have broken the law. Indeed, giving morphine in these circumstances is often good clinical practice. And yet injecting morphine into a patient is just as active a thing to do as is injecting potassium chloride. The key difference is that, in the case of potassium chloride, the *intention* is for the patient to die – and this is the means to reducing the patient's suffering. In the case of morphine the intention is to relieve the pain; an earlier death is *foreseen but not intended*. That is, at any rate, how the law in England and many other countries sees it.

On this analysis, killing, as in mercy killing, involves two aspects: that what is done is a positive act (rather than simply an omission to act); and that death is intended (and not simply foreseen). Both

43

these aspects are necessary to the definition of killing but neither by itself is sufficient.

In short, the argument to the effect that mercy killing is wrong in principle puts great moral importance on (1) the distinction between acts and omissions; and (2) the distinction between intending and foreseeing the death. Both the question of whether there is a moral, or even a conceptual, difference between acts and omissions on the one hand, or between intention and foresight on the other, have been much debated, and no single definitive position is generally agreed. The following box gives some of the thought experiments used by both sides in the argument. I do not want to discuss the general question of these moral distinctions – only where they are relevant to the euthanasia debate.

It is noteworthy that all these thought experiments involve killing, or failing to save, that is not for a person's benefit. Some of the examples, furthermore, involve killing one person to save another. In the setting of euthanasia, of course, this is not the situation. I know of no convincing thought experiment that shows a moral distinction between acts and omissions, or intention and foresight, which includes the following three key features of euthanasia:

(1) that the person whose act we are evaluating has a clear duty of care to the person who dies;
(2) that there is no issue of harming one person to benefit another;
(3) where death is in the best interests of the person who dies.

It is the harm of death that makes killing wrong

Opponents of euthanasia may ultimately rest their case on one basic principle: killing is morally wrong. They may accept that there are difficult cases when killing one person may save another – or many others. They may accept that in such circumstances killing may be the right thing to do. But in the case of euthanasia, no other person's life will be saved. The wrong of

Hypothetical cases (thought experiments) to examine the moral importance of the distinction between acts and omissions; and between intending and foreseeing an outcome

1. The cases of Smith and Jones

Smith sneaks into the bathroom of his 6-year-old cousin and drowns him, arranging things so that it will look like an accident. The reason Smith does this is that the death of his cousin will result in his coming into a large inheritance.

Jones stands to gain a similar large inheritance from the death of his 6-year-old cousin. Like Smith, Jones sneaks into the bathroom with the intention of drowning his cousin. The cousin, however, accidentally slips and knocks his head and drowns in the bath. Jones could easily have saved his cousin, but far from trying to save him, he stands ready to push the child's head back under. However, this does not prove necessary.

Is there a moral difference between Smith's and Jones's behaviour?

This pair of cases is used to support the view that there is no moral distinction between an act (killing) and an omission (failing to save) when the outcome and intention are the same.

2. The cases of Robinson and Davies

Robinson does not give £100 to a charity that is helping to combat starvation in a poor country. As a result, one person dies of starvation who would have lived had Robinson sent the money.

Davies does send £100 but also sends a poisoned food parcel for use by a charity that distributes food donations. The overall and intended result is that one person is killed from the poisoned food parcel and another person's life is saved by the £100 donation.

Is there a moral difference between what Robinson and Davies do? If there is, is this because Davies acts to kill, whereas Robinson only omits to act?

This pair of cases is used to counter the conclusion from the cases of Smith and Jones and to show that, even when the overall outcome is the same, an act (sending the poison parcel) together with the intention to kill is morally very much worse than the omission (failing to send charitable aid).

3. Sacrificing one to save five

The runaway train: A runaway train is approaching points on the railway line. If the points are not switched then the train will kill five people who are strapped to the line. If the points are switched the train will go along a different line and kill just one (different) person. There is no way of stopping the train; but you can switch the points so that one person, rather than five people, dies.

Should you switch the points?

Organ donation: One healthy person could be killed in order to use his organs to save the lives of five people with various types of organ failure.

Should you kill the healthy person and use his organs?

A common intuition is that it would be right to switch the points in the first case (so that fewer people die) but wrong to kill the healthy person in order to use his organs to save more lives. In both cases, however, by not acting five people die and by acting only one person dies. What justifies the common intuitions? This pair of examples is used in support of the view that the nature of the act can make enormous moral difference even when the outcome is the same.

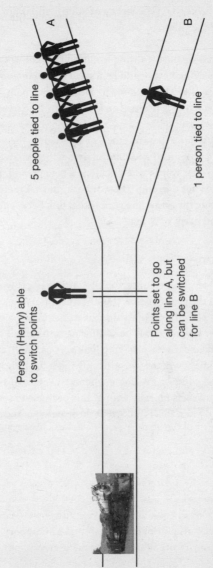

5 people tied to line A

1 person tied to line B

Person (Henry) able to switch points

Points set to go along line A, but can be switched for line B

1. If Henry does nothing, the train will run along line A and kill five people. If Henry switches the points, the train will run along line B and kill one (different) person. The train cannot be stopped in time, nor can any of the six people tied to a rail track be released in time. Should Henry switch the points?

euthanasia is based on the wrong of killing, and is not balanced by saving any other life.

It is right that we have a strong intuition that killing is wrong. For most people dying now would be a great harm compared with continuing to live. The reason why killing is normally a great wrong is that dying is normally a great harm. The wrong of killing, however, is a result of the harm of dying, not vice versa. If, therefore, it is in the best interests of a patient to die now rather than suffer a prolonged and painful dying, then killing is no longer a wrong. In other words when death is a benefit, and not a harm, then killing is not a wrong. Those who argue that mercy killing is wrong in principle forget the conceptual link between the wrong of killing and harm of dying.

Conclusion

I reject the view that voluntary active euthanasia is wrong in principle on the grounds that this argument puts the cart before the horse: it is the harm of dying that makes killing a wrong and not the other way round. When suffering is the result of following a moral principle then we need to look very carefully at our moral principle and ask whether we are applying it too inflexibly. I believe this is what we are doing when we claim that voluntary active euthanasia is morally wrong. It is perverse to seek a sense of moral purity when this is gained at the expense of the suffering of others.

Chapter 5
Do nuclear weapons make the world a safer place?

The following text is extracted from *Nuclear Weapons: A Very Short Introduction* by Joseph M. Siracusa

Does the spread of nuclear weapons make the world safer or more dangerous? Most people usually have an instinctive reply to this question: Of course, it makes things more dangerous. How could it not? It might seem surprising, therefore, that not all nuclear analysts agree, and the debate remains unresolved. Like so many of the issues relating to nuclear weapons, the debate is built largely on speculation and ambiguous historical experience. Nuclear weapons remain attractive to insecure or ambitious states. In regional rivalries such as the subcontinent, East Asia, and the Middle East, the bomb still has influence. Whatever else one has to say – and presumably not much has been left unsaid about the nuclear strategy of the past six decades – nuclear status still imparts extraordinary prestige and power. The nine current members of the nuclear weapon club still possess about 27,000 operational nuclear weapons of various types between them. At least another 15 countries have on hand enough highly enriched uranium for a nuclear weapon.

Since 1945, many influential voices have expressed alarm that the spread of nuclear weapons will inevitably lead to world destruction. So far, that prediction has not been proved right. But is that because of effective efforts to stop the spread of nuclear weapons, or, to borrow a phrase from former Secretary of State

Dean Acheson, after the Cuban Missile Crisis, just 'plain dumb luck'?

Nuclear proliferation remains urgent not just because of the risk of a terrorist organization getting its hands on nuclear weapons, but because the proliferation of weapons necessarily means a proliferation of nuclear deterrents. Nuclear weapons have long been a force multiplier, able to make up for imbalances in conventional military power. Paradoxically, then, the unassailable lead of the United States in military power and technology might actually invite other nations to acquire the bomb as a way to influence or even deter American foreign policy initiatives. The lesson of the first Gulf War, one Indian general was reported as saying, is that you do not go to war with the United States without the bomb, the 2003 invasion of Iraq serving as yet another glossy advertisement of the protective power of a nuclear arsenal. This is not a new development. It is, in fact, a lesson American policymakers have been concerned about for some time, and one for which no easy solution seems likely. Bill Clinton's Secretary of Defense, Les Aspin, outlined the problem in December 1993:

> During the Cold War, our principal adversary had conventional forces in Europe that were numerically superior. For us, nuclear weapons were the equalizer. The threat to use them was present and was used to compensate for our smaller numbers of conventional forces. Today, nuclear weapons can still be the equalizer against superior conventional forces. But today it is the United States that has unmatched conventional military power, and it is our potential adversaries who may attain nuclear weapons.

Accordingly, Aspin concluded, the United States could wind up being the equalized. To take an earlier example, John F. Kennedy acknowledged in the wake of the Cuban Missile Crisis that even a small number of nuclear weapons could deter even the most powerful states.

A central element of the proliferation debate revolves around the perceived effectiveness of nuclear deterrence. If deterrence works reliably, as optimists argue, then there is presumably less to be feared in the spread of nuclear weapons. But if nuclear deterrence does not work reliably, pessimists maintain, more nuclear weapons states will presumably lead not just to a more complicated international arena but a far more dangerous one.

Some analysts have made a compelling case that the fear of nuclear proliferation, or the spread of nuclear weapons, has been exaggerated. Some go even further and argue that proliferation may actually increase global stability. It is an argument peculiar to nuclear weaponry, as it does not apply and is not made with regard to other so-called weapons of mass destruction such as chemical and biological weapons. Nuclear weapons are simply so destructive, this school of thought argues, that using them is such a high bar that it would be madness itself to launch against a nuclear-armed foe. Put another way, nuclear states should know better than to fight wars with each other. The argument that proliferation is not necessarily a dire threat has been made in expansions both lateral – to other countries – and vertical – in the growth of nuclear stockpiles. 'Since 1945', remarked Michael Mandelbaum, 25 years ago, 'the more nuclear weapons each has accumulated, the less likely, on the whole, it has seemed that either side would use them'. Others have made similar arguments. Kenneth Waltz maintains, for example, that nuclear weapons preserve an 'imperfect peace' on the subcontinent between India and Pakistan. Responding to reports that all Pentagon war games involving India and Pakistan always end in a nuclear exchange, Waltz argues that 'Has everyone in that building forgotten that deterrence works precisely because nuclear states fear that conventional military engagements may escalate to the nuclear level, and therefore they draw back from the brink?'

It was an idea frequently debated during the Cold War. French military strategist General Pierre Gallois observed in 1960 that the path to greater stability lay in the increased proliferation. 'Few people are able to grasp that precisely because the new weapons have a destructive power out of all proportion to even the highest stakes, they impose a far more stable balance than the world has known in the past', he said. 'Nor is it any easier to make people realize that the more numerous and terrible the retaliatory weapons possessed by both sides, the surer the peace ... and that it is actually more dangerous to limit nuclear weapons than to let them proliferate.' Gallois made this argument in the context of justifying the French bomb and increasing NATO nuclear capabilities. 'These', Gallois concluded, 'are the realities of our time.'

Notwithstanding a few notable proponents of the 'proliferation equals more security' argument, the weight of opinion is mainly on the other side of the ledger, heightened, especially since 9/11, that the spread of nuclear weapons is a bad thing – a very bad thing, in fact. The issues driving nuclear-armed states and even terrorist groups are no longer just political; we have also seen the obsessiveness of religious fundamentalism, which does not seem amenable either to diplomacy or humanitarian restraint. Indeed, since 9/11 the 'rules' have changed and experts suggest that there are at least some terrorists who do want to inflict mass casualties. In this context, nuclear terrorism not only represents an effort to intimidate and coerce, but also poses a critical threat to states and peoples around the world.

Political scientist Scott Sagan has also highlighted the ways in which organizations and communications can fail; for example, rather than being anomalies, accidents should be seen as an inherent part of organizations. When nuclear weapons are thrown into the mix, the risk of catastrophic accidents becomes inevitable. Moreover, Sagan holds the view that a fundamental level of risk is inherent in all nuclear weapons organizations regardless of nationality or region. Clearly, it is an element that compounds the problem of nuclear weapons in regions still embroiled by centuries-old religious, cultural, and ethnic tensions. All of these elements combine in a barely controllable milieu of states' nuclear weapons policy, a disaster waiting to happen.

Chapter 6
Is there a future for feminism?

The following text is extracted from *Feminism: A Very Short Introduction* by Margaret Walters

What is the future, or even, *is* there a future, for feminism? Is it, at least in the affluent West, needed any longer? In 1992 the American Susan Faludi argued cogently, and in chilling detail, that feminists have been experiencing what she terms a 'backlash', with women who had undoubtedly benefited from the movement – as well as men, who had perhaps also benefited, though they rarely acknowledged the fact – anxiously remarking that it had all gone too far. As Juliet Mitchell and Ann Oakley suggested in their third collection of essays, *Who's Afraid of Feminism? Seeing Through the Backlash*, feminism makes many people uncomfortable, in part because the 'whole subject of who women are and what they want challenges our division between public and private life'.

In the 20th century, 'first-wave' feminists had demanded civil and political equality. In the 1970s, 'second-wave' feminism concentrated on, and gave great prominence to, sexual and family rights for women. It is these demands, now, that have become the main target of reaction. 'The personal is the political' was a popular 1970s slogan that some contemporary feminists seem to want to reverse. The political is reduced to the *merely* personal, to questions of sexuality and family life – which, of course, also have political implications which still, and urgently, need to be considered.

Natasha Walter, in *The New Feminism* (1998), while admitting that women are 'still poorer and less powerful than men', argues that the task for contemporary feminism is to 'attack the material basis of economic and social and political inequality'. An important point – but she remains extremely vague about precisely what that attack would imply. In one interview, she remarked, as if she had come up with a new idea instead of one that had been around for decades, that 'we want to work with men to change society and not against men': 'After all, especially if things are to change in the domestic arena, that's about men taking on a fair share of domestic work as about women moving more and more out of the home.' Or again, 'we must join hands with one another and with men to create a more equal society'.

But if at one moment she criticizes the older movement for being too personal, a few pages later Walter remarks that it was too political – or, even worse, that its members were 'humourless or dowdy or celibate'. (That is certainly not the way I remember it.) She goes on to describe Margaret Thatcher as 'the great unsung heroine of British feminism', who normalized female success. But Thatcher had no interest whatsoever in women's concerns, and was notoriously unsupportive of other women politicians.

Germaine Greer's *The Whole Woman* (1999) was written partly in angry and effective response to Natasha Walter's book and its 'unenlightened complacency'. Walter, Greer argues, assumes that feminism is all about 'money, sex and fashion'. Though, she adds:

> it was not until feminists of my own generation began to assert with apparent seriousness that feminism had gone too far that the fire flared up in my belly. When the lifestyle feminists had gone just far enough, giving them the right to 'have it all', i.e. money, it would have been inexcusable to remain silent.

People are undoubtedly alarmed by the *threat* of personal change, as much as by change itself. So some cling, nostalgically, to an imaginary golden age of fixed gender identities, the dream of a relationship between a man and a woman, that, whatever its inequities, was comfortably predictable. On the other hand, others insist – in Naomi Wolf's vivid phrase – that there has been a 'genderquake', with more women than ever in powerful positions. Women, Wolf argues in *Fire with Fire* (1983), must give up what she styles 'victim' feminism, stop complaining, and embrace 'power' feminism. But, as Lynne Segal remarks, movingly, at the end of her 1999 *Why Feminism?*, the movement's most radical goal has yet to be realized:

> a world which is a better place not just for some women, but for all women. In what I still call a socialist feminist vision, that would be a far better world for boys and men, as well.

The long, and at times radically innovative, history of feminism is all too easily forgotten. When 'second-wave' feminism emerged in the late 1960s, it seemed, at the time at least, unexpected, surprising, exciting. One big difference during the years since then has been the way Western women have become much more aware of other feminisms – not just in Europe, but across the world – that, hopefully, may challenge our cherished ideas and certainties, and undermine any complacency that we may have developed.

That wider awareness is due to a number of factors. Technical advances are certainly important: the fact, for example, that feminists in different countries can now communicate quickly and effectively, share experiences and information with large numbers of people, through the Internet. Academic feminism has played an important role in this. A great many universities, certainly in most Western countries, now run courses on women's studies, and specifically on feminism. Academic research has given us extremely valuable insights into women's lives at other times and in other cultures; inviting us to think about differences, as well as about common causes. Academic theses, scholarly articles and texts, as well as conferences, have all helped disseminate important information about feminism across the world.

But there is perhaps a loss involved, which is not often addressed or even acknowledged. I often recall, affectionately, this remark by Rebecca West:

> I myself have never been able to find out precisely what feminism is.
> I only know that people call me a feminist whenever I express
> sentiments that differentiate me from a doormat or a prostitute.

All previous feminisms have had an air of excitement, of transgression, or of risk about them: sometimes the excitement of the pioneer, sometimes of the outsider challenging convention. More recently, perhaps, there has been, in addition, the excitement of rediscovering our past, but also – and therefore – of *re-inventing* something. In the late 1960s and the 1970s, women's liberation *was* exciting. We felt that we were 'making it new', that we were exploring both past and present, committing ourselves to something that was new and radical and adventurous. But the girls I talked to recently have never had any comparable experience. They seem uninterested in feminism, partly because they see it simply as an academic subject – something fed to them, which they need not discover for themselves – and it is therefore respectably dull. (Except, of course, for the high-flyers who themselves aspire to academic jobs.) Feminism has, as it were, been spoon-fed to this younger generation of women, so, perhaps naturally and even healthily, they have a sneaking yearning to be politically 'incorrect'. Rejecting academic feminism, at least, seems one way of moving forward. Re-inventing feminism in terms of their own experience may, in the long run, prove another.

But the other difficulty – and it seems to me a crucial one – is that academic feminism has developed a language that makes sense only to a closed circle of initiates. Too many women feel shut out, alienated. This is not only true of feminism, of course; this morning as I was writing this, I opened the newspaper to find an exhilarating attack by the journalist Robert Fisk on what he calls the 'preposterous', even 'poisonous', language so often used by academics in general; used even, perhaps especially, by those who address urgently important political issues. 'University teachers ... are great at networking each other but hopeless at communicating with most of the rest of the world, including those who collect their rubbish, deliver their laundry and serve up their hash browns.' He ends by jokingly quoting a famous remark by Winston Churchill: 'This is English up with which I will not put.' It would be all too easy to make the same case specifically against academic feminism.

Fisk's point is one that we ignore at our peril. If feminism is to be something living and evolving, it will have to begin by re-inventing the wheel – which in this case means finding not just new issues, but a new language. In spite of everything, I still have faith that feminism *will* take us by surprise again, that it will re-invent itself, perhaps in unforeseen ways, and in areas we have thought little about. It will almost certainly come from outside the academy, and will probably – hopefully – challenge us in ways that, as yet, we cannot even glimpse.

Chapter 7
Can life without God have meaning?

The following text is extracted from *Atheism: A Very Short Introduction* by Julian Baggini

Believing the myth that without God everything is permitted may not in itself provide people with a reason to reject atheism, since it at least opens the gates to a certain amount of potentially desirable debauchery. What is perhaps more off-putting about atheism is the idea that without God nothing has a purpose. Sure, you can do what you want because there's no divine power there to stop you, but what is the point of doing anything at all? Why do we struggle through life – and for many people life is a struggle – if it all ends in naught? 'Life's a bitch and then you die' is the nihilistic mantra of the disenchanted and disappointed who have given up belief in God and think that leaves life a vacuous tragicomedy.

To answer these concerns it is necessary to go back to basics and consider the very idea of life having a meaning or purpose. The problem is that it is often assumed that there is no problem about the meaning of life for the religious. Buy into religion and meaning comes with it free. Opt out of religion, however, and you lose meaning. This line of reasoning is very similar to that which yokes together ethics and religion. It is assumed that ethics is packaged with religion and so without religion ethics becomes problematic. This is simply not true and I will argue that it is also not true that life's meaning and purpose are pre-packaged together with religion. To do this I will look at how to understand the idea that life has meaning and purpose at all.

The designer's purpose

The French existentialist thinker Jean-Paul Sartre believed that a rejection of the idea of God left humanity with no 'essence'. He meant something quite specific by 'essence', which he explains with the example of a paper knife. A paper knife has a clear essence, he says, because it was designed with a purpose: to cut paper. In this way, its creator endows it with an essence: the essential nature of the paper knife is to cut paper.

This idea of an essence corresponds to what some people might think of as the knife's purpose. In other words, the knife has a purpose which is its function as given to it by its creator.

Sartre argued that, since God does not exist, human beings are not like paper knives, since an intelligent designer did not create them. Thus, they lack what he called an essence. Interestingly, however, he did not conclude that human life lacked purpose or meaning, for reasons that will become clear in a little while.

First, however, we need to pay some attention to this idea that purpose or meaning is endowed on something by its creator. This seems to be the idea which supports the religious view that belief in God provides one automatic answer to the question of life's meaning. If we are created by God then our purpose is simply handed to us on a plate by that God, since he made us with some purpose in mind. The analogy crops up in various forms in religious discourse. For instance, people talk a little whimsically about the Bible being God's instruction manual, there to inform his creations about what they have been made for.

The problem here, however, is that on reflection this seems to provide us only with a very unsatisfactory form of meaning in life. The knife analogy shows us why. Although it is true that the knife has meaning and purpose because of its creator, this kind of purpose is hardly significant *for the knife*. Of course, the knife has no consciousness at all, and this reinforces the point that when we ascribe a purpose to something in virtue of what it was made for, this locates the significance of that purpose with the creator or the user of the object, not in the object itself.

Consider now a hypothetical example where the created object is conscious. Imagine a dystopian future where human beings are bred in laboratories to fulfil certain functions, rather like the scenario in Aldous Huxley's *Brave New World*. Here we can imagine a person who has been created with the purpose of cleaning lavatories. If that person were to ask what the meaning or purpose of his life were, we could say, in a sense correctly, 'to clean lavatories'. But to think that by doing so we had answered the important existential question about the meaning of life would be absurd. In short, a purpose or meaning given to a creature by its creator just isn't necessarily the kind of purpose or meaning that we are looking for in life when we wonder what the point of living is *for us*. If the only point in living is to serve *somebody else*'s purposes, then we cease to be valuable beings in our own right and we merely become tools for others, like paper knives or cloned workers.

This is why a belief in a creator God does not automatically provide life with a meaning. It can, however, satisfy some people's desire for meaning in one of two ways. The first is if the person decides that they are happy just to do God's will. Serving God is a good enough purpose in life for them. This seems odd to me, since I find it hard to imagine why God would want to create creatures like us solely to serve him: it's not as though he's in need of domestic help or anything like that. It also seems unnervingly close in attitude to the people who for many centuries thought it was simply their role in life to work for the aristocracy and the upper classes. To take pride in one's lowly position and to see that as conferring meaning on one's life seems to me indicative of what Nietzsche called 'slave morality': sanctifying what is in reality an unfortunate position so as to make that place seem much more desirable than it really is. This seems to be an example of what Sartre called 'bad faith': pretending to oneself that things are other than they really are in order to avoid uncomfortable truths.

A second way out for the religious is to simply trust that God has a purpose for us which is genuinely a purpose *for us* rather than something we do *for him*. We may not know what that is but we've got eternity to find out, so what's the rush? This is a perfectly coherent position but as with much else in religion it has to be recognized that it requires the religious to take something on complete blind trust, or, as they prefer to put it, on faith. To adopt this position is to admit that the religious actually don't have any clue what the meaning or purpose of life is, but that they simply trust God has one for them. And there is still the troubling doubt that a meaning that is given to us by others isn't necessarily the kind of meaning which makes life meaningful for us. The religious just have to have faith that their purpose is not the equivalent of cleaning paradise's lavatories for eternity.

Purpose as goal

So God or no God, if life is to be really meaningful it must be so in a way which speaks to our own projects, needs, or desires and not just the purposes of whatever or whoever created us. This is why, incidentally, the theory of evolution doesn't provide life with any meaning either. Evolution tells us that the reason why we are here is, in some sense, to replicate DNA. But this is a purely external explanation of why we exist and what biological function we fulfil. This no more explains the meaning of life than saying you were conceived so that your parents could claim extra child benefit. It gives part of the causal story of why you were born; it doesn't tell you why your life is significant, if indeed it is.

If we start thinking about life's meaning independently of the purposes of a creator, a natural way to start off is by thinking about our own purposes or goals. It does seem that many people do look at life's meaning in this way. They talk about what they want to have achieved by the age of 30, 50, or 65 with the implicit assumption that reaching these goals will fulfil them and make their lives meaningful.

One interesting point to note here is that in most cases people do not have the idea that these goals or purposes were given to them by God. It is true that you sometimes hear, for example, athletes saying things like 'God put me on Earth to win the 200 metres Olympic gold medal', but most of their peers will admit that winning is something they want and does God no favours at all. In general, when people set themselves life goals they choose these goals themselves, and that is actually an important part of why those goals are meaningful for them. What people are doing is trying to achieve some form of 'self-actualization'. They set goals which they see as developing and fulfilling their potential so that they can become in a sense more than they now are. So, for example, someone with a talent for music might set goals which, if achieved, will show that they have developed their musical abilities to their fullest potential and hence that they have become a more complete or developed individual than they once were.

This idea that we can choose our own purposes and goals and thus be the authors of our own meaning is an important one and I will return to it shortly. But first we should recognize some potential problems with seeing life's meaning as comprising one or more goals we set ourselves. If we are too goal-orientated two risks confront us.

The first is that we simply do not achieve our goal. In areas such as athletics, it is inevitable that many more people fail to achieve their goals than actually do so. But if a failure to hit the target is closely linked or is even a major part of what makes life meaningful for a person, then such a failure could be personally catastrophic.

The second risk is that, having achieved our goals, life then becomes meaningless. This is actually something that does happen to some people who become very focused on one particular goal that takes many years to achieve. You will hear many a person say something like, 'I spent my whole life working towards achieving this and now that I've succeeded I don't know what to do with myself'. Often, since these people have very goal-directed personalities, the response is to set another goal and get back on the treadmill. This just highlights the problem of tying meaning too closely to goal achievement: life can never be truly satisfying except in those few moments around the achievement of each goal. At all other times, you are either working for the future goal or looking back on its past attainment.

The problem can be posed more philosophically by considering what makes anything worthwhile. For example, since I lead an exciting life, today I'm going to buy some groceries. Why would I spend valuable time doing something so boring? The reason is that I need food to eat. But why should I bother eating? Two reasons: one is that I like it and the other is that I need food to live. So why bother living? And so on.

In this simple series of 'why' questions two types of answer can be given. One explains my actions in terms of another, more fundamental goal: to get food, to live. With this kind of answer, however, it is always possible to ask a further 'why' question. Why bother eating? Why bother living? In order to put a halt to the series of why questions we have to provide a reason which is sufficient in itself and does not simply relate to some further goal or purpose. One such reason I gave is that I eat because I like it. If you were to then ask why I like it, or why I should do what I like, then you have not really understood what it means to enjoy doing something. To enjoy doing something is itself a good enough reason to do it, provided it doesn't harm others or yourself, or prevent you from doing something more important, and various other similar caveats. So if I say I enjoy eating to explain why I am tucking into a plate of aloo gobi, there is no need or sense in asking a further why question.

If we apply this principle more widely, then we can see how, if we ask why we do anything in life, eventually we have to end up with things that are valuable in themselves and are not done simply to meet some further aim or goal. If we become too goal-fixated we risk missing this vital point.

That does not mean that the achievement of goals cannot contribute to life's meaning. Goals can play a very important role in giving meaning to our lives. But they fulfil this role best if they satisfy two conditions. The first is that we find the process of achieving them itself meaningful and rewarding. That way, the time we spend working towards the goal is meaningful even if we do not finally achieve it. The second is that the achieving of the goal itself leads to something which is of enduring value to us. That way, once we have achieved our goal, we do not suddenly find our lives empty.

A further danger with thinking too much about goals and achievements is that it might make the lives of too many people seem meaningless. The fact is that many people, perhaps the majority, are not goal-directed or hungry for success. What most people want is companionship, a job they enjoy, and sufficient money for a good quality of life. Given all those things, life seems meaningful enough, since that overall package is a good in itself. Does it really make sense to ask, 'Why would you want to do a job you enjoy all day and then go home to someone you love and fill your leisure time as you please?' Isn't the person who asks such a question missing something?

Life as its own answer

We have been led to the view that life's ultimate purpose must be something which is good in itself and is not just something that serves as a link in a never-ending series of purposes. This is one reason why atheists can claim that life is more meaningful for them than it is for many religious people who see this world as a kind of preparation for the next. For these people, life isn't really valuable in itself at all. It is like a coin which can be exchanged for a good that really does count: the after-life. This merely postpones the question about what makes life worth living, however, since it doesn't tell us why life in heaven is meaningful in itself but life on Earth isn't. Once again, it seems religion does not so much provide an answer as ask us to accept on trust that an answer will be forthcoming.

Since at some stage life must become worth living for its own sake or else it has no meaning or value in itself at all, the atheist's desire to try and find what makes this life worth living rather than hoping that the next one will be better seems sensible and prudent, especially given the evidence that this is the only life we're going to get anyway.

But what makes life worth living? Any short answer will sound trite, but there really is no mystery about it. Ray Bradbury put it pithily in his short story 'And the moon be still as bright'. This tells of Martians rather than humans, but the moral of the story translates:

> The Martians realized that they asked the question 'Why live at all?' at the height of some period of war or despair, when there was no answer. But once the civilization calmed, quieted, and wars ceased, the question became senseless in a new way. Life was now good and needed no argument.

When times are hard and life is going badly, life can seem pointless. But when life is good there is no need to question. As in the example above, if one's work and home life are going well, it is in a way senseless to ask why such a life is worth living. The person living it just knows it is.

Of course this really isn't good enough as an answer in itself since it doesn't tell us what to say to others or ourselves when life isn't going well. For most of us, life is pretty much a mixed bag, and periods where everything is going just fine and dandy are quite rare and brief. But what is true about Bradbury's sentiments is that the essence of the answer can only be rooted in the fact that life can be worth living in itself, even in difficult times, and there is no need for it to serve any other purpose. Furthermore, recognizing that life is its own answer to the question of why we should live is essential if we are to confront the reality of our finitude and accommodate ourselves to it. If we pretend or imagine that life's purpose lies outside living itself, we will be searching the stars for what is underneath our feet all the time.

Hedonism

Earlier, when I gave an example of something that was worthwhile in itself, I talked about eating a good meal. That might suggest that what makes living is nothing more complex than pleasure. Pleasure is, after all, a good thing in itself, something that, if we are experiencing it, does not need any further purpose to justify it. So, if life is finite and we need to find meaning in what is good in itself in life, surely we should just devote ourselves to pleasure?

Arguably, this is the secular orthodoxy of our day. Carpe diem – seize the day – has become the motto for our times. Encouraged by the media, in editorial and in advertising, we look for new and better pleasures all the time. If you were to spend just one day deliberately trying to spot how many articles in newspapers and magazines and advertisements in all media offer the promise of greater pleasure, you'll soon lose count. This is especially true if you read men's or women's lifestyle magazines, which seem solely to offer the promise of a happier, more contented, sexually stunning you. If any of these tips actually worked, people would soon have no need to read these magazines. Yet their circulations remain stubbornly high. I think that tells us something.

What is also revealing is that we are widely reported to be in general a rather dissatisfied society. In developed Western countries, we have access to more and better sources of pleasure than our predecessors could imagine. Yet we are not a noticeably fulfilled bunch. What's gone wrong?

This apparent paradox would not surprise most of the great philosophers of ethics, all of whom have been suspicious of too great an emphasis on pleasure. The main problem, variously explained, is that pleasure is by its nature transitory. It is all very well feeling good but pleasure does not in general leave a very long-lasting afterglow. Indeed, a life devoted to pleasure can be hard work, since if one is really serious about it, then one has to make a constant effort to get more and more. The present always eludes our grasp, so pleasures of the present are from the moment they are attained doomed to slip through our fingers.

This is why a life devoted to pleasure is for most of us deeply unsatisfying. Certainly a good life has its fair share of pleasure and only the most puritan of ethicists have claimed otherwise. But contentment or satisfaction requires more than just transitory pleasure. It requires us to be living the kind of lives that make us feel satisfied even when we are not particularly enjoying ourselves. There is no formula for determining what kind of life this is, and it certainly varies considerably from person to person. For some, a hedonistic life does provide ongoing satisfaction as well as transitory pleasure. For others, a quiet, slow labour of love that to an outsider may seem quite joyless can provide deep satisfaction.

The main point here is simply that we should not be too quick to assume that if this is the only life we've got, and if life's meaning is to be found in the living of life itself, then that means we should pursue a life of pleasure. That may fit the negative stereotype of the shallow atheist who seeks intoxication with pleasure to fill the emptiness of his purposeless life, but it is as accurate a view of typical atheists as the joyless Bible-basher is of the religious believer.

Chapter 8
Is globalization slowing down?

The following text is extracted from *Globalization: A Very Short Introduction* by Manfred B. Steger

There is no doubt that 9/11 and the ensuing 'global war on terror' gave an unexpected jolt to the struggle over the meaning and the direction of globalization. As George W. Bush made clear time and again, this new war was bound to be a lengthy conflict of global proportions. Throughout his second term in office, with Iraq still not pacified, the US President continued to appeal to a global audience to support America in what he called 'the decisive military and ideological struggle of the 21st century'. This raises the final question we will consider in our examination of globalization: will the global fight against terrorism lead to more extensive forms of international cooperation and interdependence, or might it stop the powerful momentum of globalization?

On first thought, it seems highly implausible that even a protracted global war on terror could stop, or even slow down, such a powerful set of social processes as globalization. Yet, there are already some early warning signs. The implementation of more intense border controls and stringent security measures at the world's major air and seaports have made travel and international trade more cumbersome. Calls for tightening national borders and maintaining sharp cultural divisions can be heard more frequently in public discourse. Belligerent patriotic sentiments are on display all over the world. Political leaders around the world – especially those whose democratic credentials are not exactly evident – are utilizing the 'terrorism' label to stigmatize and marginalize their opponents.

A close look at modern history reveals that large-scale violent confrontations were capable of stopping and even reversing previous globalization trends. As we noted in Chapter 2, the period from 1860 to 1914 constituted an earlier phase of globalization, characterized by the expansion of transportation and communication networks, the rapid growth of international trade, and a huge flow of capital. Great Britain, then the most dominant of the world's 'Great Powers', sought to spread its political system and cultural values across the globe much in the same way the USA does today. But this earlier period of globalization was openly imperialistic in character, involving the transfer of resources from the colonized global South in exchange for European manufactures. Liberalism, Great Britain's chief ideology, translated a national, not a global, imagery into concrete political programs. In the end, these sustained efforts to engineer an 'international' market under the auspices of the British Empire resulted in a severe backlash that culminated in the outbreak of the Great War in 1914.

In an enduring study on this subject, the late political economist Karl Polanyi located the origins of the social crises that gripped the world during the first half of the 20th century in ill-conceived efforts to liberalize and globalize markets. Commercial interests came to dominate society by means of a ruthless market logic that effectively disconnected people's economic activities from their social relations. The competitive rules of the free market destroyed complex social relations of mutual obligation and undermined deep-seated norms and values such as civic engagement, reciprocity, and redistribution. As large segments of the population found themselves without an adequate system of social security and communal support, they resorted to radical measures to protect themselves against market globalization. Polanyi notes these European movements against unfettered capitalism eventually gave birth to political parties that forced the passage of protective social legislation at the national level. After a prolonged period of severe economic dislocation following the end of the Great War, such national-protectionist impulses experienced their most extreme manifestations in Italian fascism and German Nazism. In the end, the liberal dream of subordinating all nation-states to the requirements of the free market had generated an equally extreme counter-movement that turned markets into mere appendices of the totalitarian state.

The applicability of Polanyi's analysis to the current situation seems obvious. Like its 19th-century predecessor, today's version of market globalism also represents a gigantic experiment in unleashing economic deregulation and a culture of consumerism on the entire world. Like 19th-century Britain, the USA draws both admiration and contempt from regions in the world that feel themselves to be oppressed and exploited by a global logic of economic integration led by a haughty 'American Empire'. Strictly speaking, of course, the USA does not constitute an 'empire'. But one could make a reasonable case for the persistence of American imperialism as a continuous and largely informal process that started with the 17th-century expansionist settlement of the North American continent and periodically assumed more coercive expressions such as the annexation of the Hawaiian Islands, parts of Samoa, the Philippines, and Puerto Rico in the 1890s. More than a century later, however, the USA no longer exerts direct dominion or formal rule – the hallmark of any 'empire' – over conquered people under its sovereign authority. And yet, the country has emerged from the Cold War as a new kind of empire of vast wealth, peerless military power, and global cultural reach. No doubt, America has become a 'hyperpower' that considers the entire world its geopolitical sphere of influence.

After 9/11, it found itself in the historically unprecedented position of enforcing its own idea of global order – even in

unilateral fashion if it so desired. Neoconservative American
foreign policy experts began to express such sentiments when they
argued that only a muscular USA willing to accept its imperial
status was up to the task of stabilizing a world unsettled by the
actions of jihadist globalists eager to get their hands on weapons
of mass destruction. For such 'hawks', the new environment of
global insecurity presented nothing less than a clear-cut case of
'American Empire'. 'Imperial globalism' might, therefore, be an apt
characterization of this neoconservative inclination to shape the
globe in the American image by military means. Its militaristic
inclinations notwithstanding, the Bush administration
constructed its imperial globalism within the established
framework of market globalism. Although its new *National
Security Strategy of the United States* (2002; revised 2006)
contains the famous pre-emption clause, it reaffirms
unequivocally that worldwide establishment of free markets and
free trade are the 'key priorities' of American national security.
Thus, American empire and globalization are not necessarily
opposites. Imperial globalism keeps all the major claims of market
globalism with two important modifications. Claim 3, nobody is in
charge of globalization, has been altered by open declarations on
the part of the Bush administration that America stands ready to
globally enforce the allegedly self-regulating market order.
As a result, a new claim has been added to market globalism:
globalization (understood as the liberalization and global
integration of markets) requires a global war on terror.

But as we have seen in the previous chapter, the pronouncements
of imperial globalism have not gone unchallenged. It is quite
conceivable that the Al Qaeda attacks of the last years were only
the opening salvos of a widening global war waged by the US
government and its allies against a growing list of terrorist
organizations and their supporters around the world. The
escalation of such a grim backlash scenario might well put the
brakes on globalization.

On the other hand, it is also possible that the ongoing efforts to contain these violent forces of jihadist globalism might actually increase international cooperation and encourage the forging of new global alliances. In order to eradicate the social causes of terrorism, the global North might be willing to replace the dominant neoliberal version of globalization with a substantive reform agenda designed to reduce the existing disparities in global wealth and well-being. Unfortunately, despite their encouraging reassurances to put a 'human face' on their predatory version of globalization, many market globalists have remained within the parameters of their corporate agenda. If implemented at all, their proposed 'reforms' have remained largely symbolic in character.

For example, in the wake of the justice-globalist demonstrations, representatives of the wealthy countries joined the WTO Secretary General in assuring audiences worldwide that they would be willing to reform the economic institution's rules and structure in the direction of greater transparency and accountability. Yet, several years later, no concrete steps have been taken to honour these commitments. Granted, the WTO has been holding special General Council sessions to comply with the urgent requests of developing countries to review several of its questionable procedures. Yet, the spokespersons of the powerful governments in the global North that dominate the WTO have made it clear that they consider existing arrangements as legally binding. In their view, procedural problems can only be addressed in the context of a new, comprehensive round of multilateral negotiations conducted according to the very rules that are being contested by many developing countries and justice-globalist NGOs.

This strategy of fortifying the market-globalist paradigm with a new rhetoric of mild reformism might work for a relatively short period. But in the long run, the growth of global inequality and the persistence of social instability harbours the potential to unleash reactionary social forces that dwarf even those responsible for the suffering of millions during the 1930s and 1940s. Indeed, as recent developments have shown, globalization's very survival will depend on humanity's ability to tackle the three major global issues confronting us in the 21st century: global climate change, increasing economic inequality, and escalating political and social violence. In order to prevent a further escalation of the violent confrontation between market globalism and its ideological opponents, world leaders must design and implement a comprehensive Global New Deal that builds and extends genuine networks of solidarity around the world.

Without doubt, the years and decades ahead will bring further challenges. Humanity has reached yet another critical juncture. Lest we are willing to let global problems fester to the point where violence and intolerance appear to be the only realistic ways of confronting our unevenly integrating world, we must link the future course of globalization to a profoundly reformist agenda. As I have emphasized in the Preface of this book, there is nothing wrong with greater manifestations of social interdependence that emerge as a result of globalization. However, these transformative social processes must have a moral compass and an ethical polestar that guide our collective efforts: the building of a truly democratic and egalitarian global order that protects universal human rights without destroying the cultural diversity that is the lifeblood of human evolution.

Chapter 9
What is the future of sex?

The following text is extracted from *Sexuality: A Very Short Introduction* by Véronique Mottier

Since the late 1980s, sexuality has figured prominently on Western political agendas, covering national as well as international issues. Controversies around teenage pregnancy rates, prevention of sexually transmitted disease, regulation of prostitution, sexual exploitation of children, Internet porn, gays and lesbians in the military, gay 'marriage' and adoption, hate crimes, new reproductive technologies, and the 'private' morality of politicians are the topic of intense public debate, and older issues such as access to abortion are currently subjected to renewed contestation. Issues such as Aids, sex tourism, international trafficking of women, and Internet networks of paedophiles illustrate the global nature of politics of sexuality, as well as the resurgence of moral purity discourses and their political influence. Against the backdrop of the politics of sexuality, as well as wider social and technological developments, sexuality has undergone profound changes over the past few decades. Modern sexual science has documented the impact of such changes on individual practices. Somewhat ironically, the primary agents in the transformation of sexual truths and relations of power are those that medicine and sexology had constructed as marginal in relation to hegemonic male heterosexuality, namely women and homosexuals of both sexes, as we have seen throughout this volume.

In the process, social understandings of sexuality have opened up to a plurality of meanings. Whereas liberation theorists saw sexual pleasure as crucial for the fulfilment of full human potential and happiness, competing understandings have portrayed sexuality as the site of risk, death, moral decay, commercial exploitation, male violence, political self-affirmation, and destabilization of identities.

Liquid sex

Modern individuals can in principle adopt sexual identities at will, but they do not do so in conditions of their own choosing. The social and political context of modernity sets the stage for sexual possibilities. For example, new communication technologies such as the Internet provide new sexual options, including the adoption of 'virtual' identities in cyberspace as well as greater access to potential partners. The modern world, as the sociologist Zygmunt Bauman argues in his book *Liquid Love*, is characterized by fluidity in social relations generally, encouraging a reluctance towards long-term commitments since a 'better product' might be just around the corner. The fragmentation of sexual subcultures is mirrored in the specialization of the commodities on offer. Gay men's dating websites such as Gaydar have become global phenomena, with users including men from countries such as Algeria, Afghanistan, Pakistan, or the Democratic Republic of Congo. More specialized dating agencies cater for 'heterosexual, gentile (non-Jewish), whites only', 'gay black females', or the 'unhappily married/attached', while the now defunct Safe Love International, which included prominent sexologists such as Theresa Crenshaw on its advisory council, promised that its members were 'Aids-free'.

Citizens of the modern sexual world make sense of their personal identities and problems in new ways, as reflected in a recent dilemma submitted to the popular internationally syndicated

Internet relationship and sex advice column 'Savage Love', run by American gay author of *Skipping Towards Gomorrah* (2002) Dan Savage:

> For the past 15 years, I've identified as bisexual: I've been in monogamous relationships with men and women. I married a wonderful guy a few years ago. However, I recently realised that I identify as gay. I've talked to my husband about this, and he's okay with it. I decided to stay with him and remain monogamous. We have a great relationship – and great sex. We left open the possibility of me taking a female lover in the future, if needed. For now, I'm happy with him. I flirt with girls, we talk openly about my preferences, but I haven't had sex with a woman since before I married him. And I'm okay with that. So, here's my dilemma: Is it right to call myself a lesbian if I'm married to (and sexually involved with) a man? I hesitate to stay with the 'bi' label, since I have no interest in other men. Can I call myself a lesbian even though I'm not sleeping with women?

Advice columns, agony aunts, therapists, support groups such as Sex Addicts Anonymous, self-help books, and sex manuals can be drawn upon to offer advice on relationship rules, sexual etiquette, and sexual mechanics in the liquid world of modern sex. Titles such as *Women Who Love Too Much*, *Relationship Rescue*, *How to Fall Out of Love*, or *If It Hurts, It Isn't Love* guide readers through the minefield of intimacy and emotions. Other works privilege a more practical angle, such as *Sexercise* ('will help you get fit while you're having fun!'), *This Book Will Get You Laid* ('the bonking bible no bloke should be without'), or American sexologist Dr Ruth's *Sex for Dummies*. Specific subgroups are catered for by works such as *The Adventurous Couple's Guide to Strap-On Sex*, *The Gay Joy of Sex*, *Sex: A Man's Guide*, *The New Love and Sex After 60*, *The Lesbian Sex Book*, or *Enabling Romance: A Guide to Love, Sex and Relationships for People with Disabilities (and for the People Who Care About Them)*.

Best-selling self-help books such as *The Rules: Time-Tested Secrets for Capturing the Heart of Mr. Right* (1995) reproduce traditional norms of female and male sexual behaviour and needs, based upon the claim that men and women are biologically different creatures. 'In a relationship, the man must take charge. He must propose. We are not making this up – biologically, he's the aggressor', as the *Rules*, such as 'don't talk to a man first (and don't ask him to dance)', formulate it.

Attempts to break away from dominant norms frequently involve the formulation of new normativities, however, as illustrated by Shere Hite's emphasis on the necessity for women to experience sexual pleasure:

> If you can't orgasm, you could also read books on sex therapy, feminist literature, and try to talk to friends about how they have orgasms. You could also try a local women's self-help group, perhaps a sex-therapist, or a lover who was sensitive enough to help. Don't give up. Many women have learned to orgasm after years of not knowing how, and it is never too late to discover what works for you.

The current transformations and politics of sexuality have started to problematize the hegemony as well as the forms of 'normality'. Feminist critiques of sexuality have encouraged wider understandings of sexuality, less centred on penetrative intercourse alone, while gay and lesbian communities of choice and attendant political activism have publicly demonstrated the profound transformations of both the sexual order and the gender order of the West in recent decades.

In their radical experiments with intersections between gender and sexuality, the 'queers' queers' are perhaps the sexual revolutionaries of our time. Just as self-castrating early Christians, anarchist free-lovers, 1960s swingers, Reichian sexual liberationists, and political lesbians came from the periphery of the continent of sex to invent new meanings and practices, so the pomosexual 'lesbian separatist who becomes a professional dominatrix, then falls in love with a male-to-female transsexual girl, decides to go through with a sex change, becomes a guy, and realizes he's a gay man' questions our most basic assumptions about gender and sexual identity, and illustrates the possibilities for greater fluidity that the (post)modern world offers.

Does that mean that, in future, we will all think of ourselves as pomosexuals? Are we currently witnessing the final death throes of heterosexuality and homosexuality? As we have seen, current sexual 'truths' and identities are relatively recent historical constructs, produced by sexual science and medicine. The future of sex may well involve leaving behind the constraints of 19th-century 'sexuality'. Theorists of sexuality have thus called for collective 'un-sexualization'. At the same time, there is little in the current state of the politics of sexuality to lead us to conclude that an 'unsexual' future is anywhere near, given the renewed propping up of traditional understandings of sex by the fundamentalist backlash, as well as by scientific discourses. What is certain, however, is that alternative futures of sex based on moral pluralism cannot escape new normativities, new relations of power, and new state policies. No culture can have 'full' sexual freedom. As the sociologist Ken Plummer puts it:

> However neutral and objective talk about sexual diversity appears to be, it is also talk about power. Every culture has to establish – through both formal and informal political processes – the range and scope of the diversities that will be outlawed or banned.

As I have argued, sexual needs, values, and emotions are the products of specific historical contexts. Current practices may contribute to undermining concepts of 'sexuality', but, whatever changes scientific and technological developments will bring to our bodies and relationships, future meanings of sex will be shaped by society and politics.

Chapter 10
What is the economic impact of immigration?

The following text is extracted from *International Migration: A Very Short Introduction* by Khalid Koser

The economic impact of immigration

The economic impact of immigration in destination societies is a hotly contested field. Academic debates are, on the whole, more sophisticated in the USA than Europe, partly because until recently the political and economic climate in Europe has made it difficult to argue the case for the positive economic benefits of immigration. This was not always the case; the logic behind the *gastarbeiter* system in Germany during the 1950s and 1960s, for example, was almost entirely one of economic benefits.

The primary debate has been about the impact of immigration on economic growth, and it is still ongoing and unresolved. According to George Borjas, probably the world's leading economist of migration, 'while recent theoretical work has made strides towards explaining the possible links between immigration and growth, only a few empirical studies have been conducted, and no clear picture has emerged from these' (*Journal of Economic Perspectives*, 9/2 (1995), 39).

Proponents that the impact is positive point to the willingness of migrants to take low-wage jobs, the high levels of ambition that many immigrants demonstrate, and the flexibility that comes from having a regular supply of labour. It is also argued that immigrants increase returns on capital investments, have a minimal effect on other wages, that their entrepreneurship generates jobs, and that their labour can enable a country to remain competitive in an industry that would otherwise lose out to international competition. In some cases the positive effects of migration on countries of origin is also included on this side of the debate.

Other equally respected experts in the USA and elsewhere make just as convincing a case that immigration can have a negative economic impact. They point to higher levels of unemployment among the foreign-born, the prevalence of large family sizes with the attendant welfare costs, and the negative effects of competition with established minorities. A pool of low-skilled

Historical experiences

Several episodes in recent history provide interesting precedents for assessing the economic impacts of immigration. In 1962, 900,000 people of European origin living in Algeria moved to France, increasing the French labour force by 1.6 per cent. Analysis found that at most the impact was to reduce wages in the regions where they settled by 0.8 per cent and raise the unemployment rate by 0.2 percentage points. In 1974, 600,000 colonists returned to Portugal from the African colonies of Angola and Mozambique. Empirical analysis was unable to discern any impact on the labour market. In 1980 around 125,000 Cubans entered Miami, increasing the labour force by 7 per cent. When the impact of their immigration on resident unskilled labour from different ethnicities was assessed, only the Cubans appeared to have been negatively affected.

(UNDESA, World Economic and Social Survey: International Migration, New York: UN, 2004)

labour can also defer the restructuring and reorganization of industries; it can create sweatshop labour conditions and undercut the power of trade unions to maintain labour standards.

Within the general debate on the economic impact of migration, three aspects have attracted particular attention, namely impacts on the availability of jobs for the native-born and on the level of their wages, and fiscal effects, especially on public sector costs.

One of the most abiding fears expressed in destination countries around the world is that migrants will take away jobs from the

Self-employed foreign workers and ethnic entrepreneurs

There is a growing literature on self-employed foreign workers, who are numerous in Canada, Denmark, Finland, Spain, Ireland, and the UK. Three main explanations for high levels of self-employment among immigrants in such countries are common. One is based on the selective nature of migration, that immigrants are more dynamic and less reluctant to take risks than the native-born. Another argument, conversely, is that migrants become self-employed because of barriers to securing salaried jobs, including discrimination, language obstacles, and poor access to information. The development of economic activities aimed at immigrants' communities of origin is a third explanation, and the concept of ethnic entrepreneurship is often used to describe these community-type activities. Importantly, their impact often extends beyond a specific ethnic community, for example, Indian, Italian, and Turkish culinary specialities were largely introduced by immigrants for immigrants but are now an integral part of eating habits all over the world.

native-born. This concern is especially evident in many European countries, where unemployment levels are relatively high and the proportion of long-term unemployed among the unemployed relatively large. In reality, however, this appears to be rarely the case. That is because in most countries in the world migrants are admitted to fill gaps in the local labour market (this is not true for refugees who are admitted on the basis of humanitarian not economic criteria). These can be skills gaps which the local training and education system has been unable to fill, or low-status jobs that locals are unwilling to do. Migrant workers are rarely encouraged to enter situations to compete directly with local workers. Extensive comparative research across the industrialized nations indicates that the impact of immigration on jobs for local populations is at worst neutral and at best positive in that it can create economic growth and more jobs.

A key aspect of the immigration debate in the USA has focused on the impact on wage levels. At a national and aggregate level, the consensus that has emerged is that negative effects are most likely to be felt for those whose labour market characteristics are most like migrants, in other words for those who are in direct competition with migrants for work. This effect, it is argued, is offset by positive effects on the wages for those who are not competing with migrants for work because they benefit from the greater profitability of US firms as a result of immigration.

With the growth in the US of low-skilled migration in recent years, attention has focused in particular on the effects of immigration on the wages of native-born low-skilled workers. African Americans are over-represented among the less skilled and are highly vulnerable within the labour market as a whole, so the possible effects of immigration on them are especially salient. The results of recent research are not entirely clear or consistent. On the one hand, studies conducted in New York have shown a declining relative position for African American males in terms of labour market participation and earnings in the 1980s and early

1990s, at exactly the same time that the highest levels of immigration were recorded, much of it involving the low-skilled. On the other hand, few studies have been able to demonstrate a net effect that can be attributed solely to immigration. In other words, immigration is normally one of a variety of factors that might account for the depression of wages, and it is hard to isolate its effect.

A final aspect of the debate on the economic impact of immigration concerns its effect on public finances. Separate studies in Australia, Germany, the UK, and the USA have found the overall effect to be positive; that on aggregate immigrants generate more in taxes paid than they cost in services received. The normal explanations are that there is a skewed age structure within most migrant communities which are dominated by people of an economically active age, and in general there are high levels of employment among migrants. In addition, the destination country has not normally had to bear the cost of rearing, educating, and training the migrants. In many cases, furthermore, they do not have to bear the cost of old age dependency either, as migrants often return home when they retire.

There are important variations. Studies suggest, for example, that the fiscal impact of immigration is less clearly positive in countries like the USA which do not face an acute ageing population problem, as compared with many European countries and Japan which do. A study in New Zealand found that, while overall immigration makes a positive fiscal contribution of NZ\$ 3,240 to government revenues, new migrants from Asia and the Pacific Islands specifically cost more than they contribute in taxes.

A key factor in all the above aspects of the debate on the economic impacts of immigration is the extent to which immigrants are employed, and there are some important variables. In the USA, but also in Europe, a particular feature of recent debates has been the argument that the character of international migration has changed. Family reunion means there is a larger proportion of economically inactive migrants. There are also increasing numbers of asylum-seekers who are not permitted to work legally for a certain period. More generally it has been suggested that new waves of migrants show less capacity to achieve social mobility and skill acquisition than earlier arrivals.

The overall employment rate of the foreign-born population in the EU 25 is lower, at 61 per cent, than that of the EU average. This rate varies significantly, however, according to place of origin. Immigrants from Western and Southern Europe have higher employment rates than the EU average, whereas those from other parts of the world have lower employment rates. Unemployment is particularly high among immigrants from Turkey, the Middle East, and Africa. There is also a strong gender difference. While foreign-born men have only a slightly lower employment rate than the EU average for men, foreign-born women have very significantly lower employment rates.

It is also important to note that local and city-level studies do not necessarily yield the same conclusions on immigrant employment and fiscal effects as national studies. At the local government level in a number of major European cities, for example, the net effect of immigrants on public sector budgets has been found to be negative, largely because of high levels of unemployment within certain immigrant communities. Research by William Clark in the nine main entry-point cities for new migrants in the USA demonstrates a fall in skills and income and increases in poverty and dependency relative to the native-born, a gap that has grown over time. Further analysis by Clark suggests that these problems are specifically associated with certain locales and certain ethnic and national groups. Unskilled Mexican migrants in Los Angeles County, for example, were found to be particularly impoverished.

It is important to conclude this section with one final observation. This is that there is often a gap between the findings of academic research such as that cited here, and public and even political opinions. Even where research points unambiguously to the conclusion that immigrants contribute to economic growth, do not compete for jobs, do not lower wages for the native-born, and represent good value in cost-benefit terms, this is not how they will necessarily be viewed. In the USA and Europe there has consistently found to have been a correlation between negative public opinion on the scale of immigration and high unemployment levels, even where no direct relationship between the two can be established. Similarly in Malaysia and South Africa, for example, immigration is regularly blamed for unemployment.

Chapter 11
Is privacy a fundamental human right?

The following text is extracted from *Human Rights: A Very Short Introduction* by Andrew Clapham

The notion of privacy forces us to confront fundamental issues at the heart of human rights. Although there is a popular perception that 'time-honoured' rights to privacy are now constantly under attack, it is not at all clear where the notion of privacy came from. If we trace the origin of the concept, we find that privacy is not a traditional constitutional right; one does not find 18th-century revolutionary demands for privacy. In fact, the protection of privacy seems to have developed in an *ad hoc* way in response to feelings of outrage or embarrassment as the need arose. In human rights law, privacy has become a residual right, used to buttress claims that might otherwise be based on respect for dignity, home, correspondence, sexuality, identity, or family. Some might suggest that privacy is a *natural* demand and references are often made to religious texts, which suggest that from ancient times it has been clear that human beings should shield their private parts from public view. But the fact that many people accept that some things, such as nudity, going to the toilet, and sexual activity, should take place in private, rather than in public, does not really help to define where a universal right to privacy comes from, or what it is supposed to protect.

An early reference to a right to privacy can be found in an 1881 case in the United States which arose out of a complaint by a woman that she had been observed against her will during childbirth. Although her complaint succeeded as a case of battery, the court referred to her 'right to the privacy of her apartment'. Further impetus for the right came in the form of a US law review article by Louis Brandeis and Samuel Warren in 1890, called 'The Right to Privacy'. It may be that the inspiration to write the article stemmed from the unwelcome publicity surrounding the wedding of Warren's daughter. In any event, 19th-century preoccupations centred on unauthorized observation or publication. The case studies used by Brandeis and Warren included: an English court's injunction for breach of confidence restraining distribution of etchings made by Prince Albert and Queen Victoria; a French court's protection for the family of an actress, prohibiting the circulation of reproductions of a death-bed portrait; and in Germany, the seizing of death-bed photos of Bismarck following a request by his children.

As various national laws developed to protect these interests, there was a change in the focus of what needed to be protected by the concept of privacy. By the end of the Second World War, the concerns were different. Early on, Cuba made a proposal for an article protecting privacy in the Universal Declaration of Human Rights. It included three headings: protection of honour, reputation, and correspondence. The focus on the protection of honour and dignity remains in the Inter-American system for the protection of human rights. However, the concerns of the drafters of the Universal Declaration were wider, and the eventual formulation in the Universal Declaration and subsequent treaties covers not only attacks on honour and reputation, but also interference with 'privacy, family, home or correspondence'. In addition, the scope of this protection has been further defined to protect certain aspects of human dignity, which we shall examine in detail below.

Articulating the duties that correspond to this right is hard, as other rights immediately raise their heads in seeming opposition. The right to privacy may extend only to the point where it does not restrict someone else's right to freedom of expression or right to information. The scope of the right to privacy is similarly constrained by the general interest in preventing crime or in promoting public health. However, when we move away from the property-based notion of a right (where the right to privacy would protect, for example, images and personality), to modern notions of private and family life, we find it harder to delimit the right. This is, of course, the strength of the notion of privacy, in that it can adapt to meet changing expectations and technological advances.

In sum, *what* is privacy today? The concept encompasses a claim that we should be unobserved, and that certain information and images about us should not be circulated without our permission. *Why* did these privacy claims arise? They arose because powerful people took offence at such observation. Furthermore, privacy was assimilated to the need to protect the family, home, and correspondence from arbitrary interference and, in addition, there has been a determination to protect honour and reputation. *How* is privacy protected? Historically, privacy was protected by restricting circulation of the damaging material. But if the concept of privacy first became interesting legally as a response to reproductions of images through etchings, photography, and newspapers, more recent technological advances, such as data storage, digital images, DNA identification, retina scans, and the internet, pose new threats to privacy. The right to privacy is now being reinterpreted to meet those challenges.

We might identify at least five contemporary dimensions to privacy. First, there is a desire to be free from observation. We have already mentioned the sense that some of us want to be shielded from others when we are undressed. From this, rights may flow with regard to strip searches, detention, medical situations, hidden cameras, and other forms of surveillance. Second, there is a desire to restrict circulation of information and images about ourselves, especially where knowledge about such information could be embarrassing or prejudicial to our interests. Third, there is an interest in being able to communicate with others without third parties eavesdropping or monitoring our communications. Although the original protection in the human rights treaties covered 'correspondence', the scope of privacy protection has been extended to challenge telephone tapping, monitoring of the sorts of calls made, and most recently, employers' scrutiny of employees' emails. Fourth, our physical and mental well-being needs protection. The law of privacy has been developed to guarantee protection from domestic violence, sexual abuse, corporal punishment, and environmental hazards. Fifth, it is felt that space should be made so that we can develop our personalities free from control. If we are not free to make certain choices about sex, identity, and association then we may fail to develop our personalities to their full potential. In this way, international human rights treaties have been successfully used to challenge laws that criminalized consensual homosexual activity.

But the concept of privacy has another side. Privacy has been used to shield violence against women from interference by law enforcement officials. Privacy has also been invoked as a justification for racial discrimination when hiring domestic staff or excluding people from membership of clubs and associations. The concept of a private sphere free from governmental interference has meant that issues of marital rape, child abuse, and female genital mutilation were not seen as part of the human rights debate, and that dealing with these issues meant invading someone's privacy.

These problems have been compounded by the notion of a public/private divide in law. Many legal systems have evolved around the idea that public law (including human rights protection) should regulate issues concerning governmental authorities, whilst private law regulates disputes between private entities that are not connected to the state or local authorities. By implication, it is sometimes said that private matters are not the business of the public authorities. According to this line of argument, concerns relating to human dignity in this private sphere cannot therefore be remedied through state intervention or recourse to human rights law. Furthermore, to compound this exclusionary policy, international human rights law has been developed through the consideration of *states'* obligations under the various treaties. Because courts and committees can usually only hear complaints against governments, an assumption has arisen that all violations of human rights require the involvement of the government. Violations in the private sphere were simply not considered to be covered by international human rights law.

This has changed. First, the international bodies established under the human rights treaties have interpreted governments' obligations as giving rise to duties to protect individuals even from attacks on their rights by private individuals and other non-state entities. These obligations are often known as positive obligations, or obligations to protect. Second, the development of the law of international crimes has highlighted questions of individual responsibility for violations of international law. The fact is that some of the worst atrocities the international community has to deal with take place without any question of governmental involvement. Obvious examples include the rapes, torture, and civilian massacres carried out by rebel groups. There is now a good argument that such non-state actors have certain human rights obligations. In turn, the scope of human rights obligations is coming to be seen as having an impact on other non-state actors, such as the United Nations and NATO (in the context of their peace operations), international financial institutions (such as the World Bank and the International Monetary Fund), multinational corporations and other forms of businesses, and all sorts of political parties, religious groups, unions, clubs, and associations.

The traditional distinction between public and private, and the consequent exclusion of domestic and family matters from the public sphere, has led to a careful feminist critique of the construction of the public/private divide and its implications for women and women's rights. It has sometimes been suggested that abolishing the notion of a public/private divide is essential to ensure that oppression in the private sphere would be tackled as a matter of public political concern. In particular, it is clear that the human rights discourse traditionally focused on a public sphere and 'forgot' the concerns of women in fields such as armed conflict, development, the workplace, and the family. The solution, however, is not to abolish the right to privacy: privacy claims have proven effective to ensure a degree of control over one's body, one's sexual relations, and over personal information. The way forward is to take women's claims seriously and acknowledge that human rights apply in the private sphere.

Balancing privacy and other values

Balancing the right to privacy with the competing right to freedom of expression is certainly contextual, one might even say cultural. Although the stakes may seem small to some, the example of a newspaper claiming freedom to publish photographs of a famous person with her children helps us to understand the issues. Human rights simultaneously claim to protect freedom of expression and the right to privacy. How to choose? Here we have to admit that the human rights framework is not akin to a set of traffic regulations or simple road rules. There is plenty of room for different people, different judges even, to come to different conclusions, and again everything depends on context. But the disputes are now often argued in terms of weighing different values – and the lexicon of human rights concepts is the vocabulary called upon to articulate the principles at stake.

In a case concerning the publication of photographs of Princess Caroline of Monaco, the judges of the German Federal Constitutional Court were unsympathetic to the claims for breach of privacy – favouring instead the interests protected by press freedom. They saw the need to allow such publication as part of ensuring access to information for all. On the other hand, the judges of the European Court of Human Rights favoured the protection of the Princess's privacy.

The expansion of the concept of privacy to protect one from pollution, including noise pollution, illustrates the point that privacy is not considered an absolute right and that decision makers have a complex task in determining whether an interference with the enjoyment of this right is justified. In 2001, residents near Heathrow Airport succeeded in convincing a Chamber of the European Court of Human Rights (by five votes to two) that the noise levels at night were an unjustifiable interference with their effective enjoyment of their right to respect for their homes and their private and family lives. On appeal, the Grand Chamber held by twelve votes to five that the Government had struck the correct balance between the rights of the residents and the rights of others to travel and pursue competitive commercial operations (in turn considered necessary for the 'economic well-being' of the country). The dissenters disagreed and felt the balance had not been properly struck. As they put it:

> the close connection between human rights protection and the
> urgent need for a decontamination of the environment leads us to
> perceive health as the most basic human need and as pre-eminent.
> After all, as in this case, what do human rights pertaining to the
> privacy of the home mean if, day and night, constantly or
> intermittently, it reverberates with the roar of aircraft engines?

Protecting health as an element of privacy provides one clear dilemma when it is perceived as hindering the convenience of airline travellers and the economy.

With regards to the increasing use of closed-circuit surveillance cameras, DNA and other genetic information, the same questions we discussed earlier must be asked. Is there a legitimate aim? Are the interferences authorized by an accessible law, and are they really necessary in a democratic society to protect the community from crime and threats to national security? There are fears that such data will be used by employers and insurance companies to detect those likely to have future health problems, thus introducing an unacceptable level of discrimination based on predicted future misfortune.

The priority given to privacy depends on the context and, to some extent, the weight that a particular society or decision-making body wishes to accord such a claim. It is perhaps helpful to recall a primary purpose of protecting privacy, which is to allow for the development of the personality in relation to others without unnecessary interference. Where the protection of privacy is being invoked to shield public officials from criticism, to seal off violence in the domestic arena from official protection, or to justify racial or other types of prohibited discrimination, then we should be alert to the appropriation of the concept of privacy to assist in the denial of human rights. The right to privacy has forged important advances in the international protection of human rights – but it simultaneously remains a tool that can easily be invoked to undermine other rights. Claims that privacy is under threat are set to continue for some time; how much weight they are accorded will depend on what is considered to be at stake.

Chapter 12
Why are more women active in the Christian church than men?

The following text is extracted from *Christianity: A Very Short Introduction* by Linda Woodhead

Christianity has much to offer women. Women benefit in two ways: first, by the restraint that appeal to Christian values may place on the unbridled exercise of male power; and second, by the recognition and affirmation of the value of typically feminine roles, virtues, and dispositions.

Even though the New Testament contains no unambiguous endorsement of female equality, and certainly offers no support to female dominance, there are hints and glimmers of a 'kingdom' in which things could be different. Jesus not only ministers amongst and with women, he teaches that humility, poverty of spirit, and sincere devotion are more important than worldly power or priestly status. He speaks of a love whose exercise knows no limits or distinctions, a love which, as Paul puts it, 'is patient and kind ... not jealous or boastful ... not arrogant or rude ... does not insist on its own way ...'. Such a message could inspire and empower those whose daily work and care were often ascribed little economic or cultural, let alone spiritual, value.

Christianity could also offer women congenial social space. In theory at least, the church community is bound only by ties of love – love for one another and for the God whose Son gives His life for His church. The resonance with the ethos of the family is striking, and it is no coincidence that the image of the family should be so central to ecclesiastical self-understanding (the church as the 'family of God'). Though this image could be used to reinforce the rule of fathers, it could also have profound significance for those whose daily lives were taken up with the unrewarded tasks of loving, caring, and sacrificing for others. Women with children have much to gain from an institution like the church that supports the family, exalts the domestic role, offers support and companionship in the task of rearing and educating children, and, once children have left home, can find other caring roles for women to perform. In any case, women seem more inclined than men to join a community for the good of community and relationship alone, irrespective of any other roles or privileges that membership might bring.

What is more, for much of Christian history the church has been the only public space that women have been allowed to occupy besides the home – certainly the only one that wives and daughters might be allowed to attend independent of husbands and fathers. The later medieval period saw a flourishing of female piety, still evident in the rich flowering of feminized art and sculpture that occurred at that time, in which images of female saints abound. Despite Protestantism's hostility to such images, some post-Reformation churches offered women new opportunities for education, literacy, and even public ministry. In the 19th century, missionary work and charitable activities offered women an outlet for energies and ambitions that would otherwise have been frustrated. Though the avowed aim of (for example) female-led temperance movements might be to curb the consumption of alcohol, the deeper concern was often to bridle men and machismo – male spending, male sexuality, and male violence. Even though it could not be made explicit, such organizations sometimes harboured elements of a feminist agenda. Churchmen might have become worried about such activities, but it was hard to control women who claimed to be carrying out the injunctions of Christ. Though the scriptures had more often been used to justify male control of women, it was possible for the tables to be turned.

But even if Christianity can attract women by affirming feminine virtue and providing congenial social space and tools of resistance to masculine domination, does not its close association of masculinity and divinity have the opposite effect? Not necessarily. In fact, women may be more attracted to the worship of a male God and saviour than men, and the reason is not hard to see. If society encourages women to love, serve, obey, and even worship men, then it is not difficult to transfer such attitudes to a male God – or for devotion to a male God to reinforce such behaviours. Indeed, in so far as society reinforces heterosexuality, it is much more natural for a woman to offer intense, emotional devotion to a male deity than for a man to do the same. Whilst men may have no difficulty in bowing down before the power, majesty, and fatherly authority of God, they are less likely than women to 'give their hearts to Jesus' or enter into an intense, emotional relationship with him. We noted the development of romantic, erotic forms of mystical piety in earlier chapters. 'Brides of Christ' would surrender to Christ the heavenly bridegroom and feel themselves melting into him. Such imagery is not confined to the past. In many Biblical and Charismatic Christian circles today women still engage in romance with Christ, and still affirm – to quote one Evangelical 'bride' – that 'Jesus alone understands me, forgives me and loves me'.

Such erotic piety may have different social and personal implications. It may reinforce patriarchal norms and encourage women to accept forms of male domination to which they would not otherwise be willing to submit. It may offer women a means of coping with such domination, but prevent them from questioning the social order of which it is a part. Or it may equip them with an effective means of resisting male domination and constructing different social arrangements. In Catholicism, for example, 'brides of Christ' could – and still can – escape earthly marriage altogether by entering a convent where they gather with like-minded women and may attain considerable independence from men.

In the context of patriarchal societies, Christianity may therefore appeal to women *because* of its masculine bias, rather than in spite of it. Christianity may have much to offer women who wish to turn their backs on power and embrace the virtues of love, humility, powerlessness, and self-sacrifice. But it also has a considerable amount to offer those who want some share in such power. For if power is concentrated in a male God and His church, there is much more to be gained by joining it than by rejecting it. Not only could Christian women claim the protection of the Almighty Father God, they could also enter into a relationship with Him that was every bit as close and intense as that enjoyed by a man. By such means a handful of women in Christian history have claimed the right to do theology, to speak for themselves, even to command kings and popes; in the societies in which they lived it is hard to imagine any other route by which they could have done so.

The contemporary situation

Christianity can no longer take male domination for granted, for the societies in which it is situated have been changing – particularly in the West. Of the several unprecedented changes that took place in advanced industrial societies in the last quarter of the 20th century, the move towards gender equality has been one of the most significant. Whilst genuine equality remains an elusive ideal, as an ideal at least it is now widely accepted. A recent survey of cultural values worldwide indicates that such acceptance is now the single most important cultural item separating affluent Western societies from less economically developed countries in the rest of the world. The difference can be traced back not only to cultural and educational differences, but to the much greater scarcity of resources outside the West. Where money and jobs are in short supply, men have always been more likely to try to preserve a monopoly than when they have nothing to lose by allowing women (relatively) free access to the labour market.

Of the many threats that Christianity has to face in modern times, gender equality is one of the most serious, though perhaps the most underestimated by the churches. The more radical feminists had Christianity in their sights from the start. When Elizabeth Cady Stanton (1815–1902) set out to liberate women from their traditional shackles, for example, one of her first projects was a *Woman's Bible* in which the passages used by men to keep women in subjection were highlighted and critiqued. Although some early campaigners for female emancipation belonged to the churches, and though some church-related movements helped nurture women's entrance onto the public stage, the campaigners who embraced the feminist cause most wholeheartedly nearly always made a break from Church and Biblical Christianity (Mystical Christianity sometimes proved more compatible with feminism).

The rift between Christianity and feminism was exacerbated not so much by the churches' opposition to the cause, but by their general indifference. Even churches that supported the emancipation of slaves, the amelioration of the condition of the industrial working class, and the civil rights movement of the 1960s often failed to give similar support to the cause of women's liberation. So far as their own institutional life was concerned, a few of the more liberal Biblical and Mystical churches supported women's ministry as early as the late 19th century, but Church Christianity and conservative Biblical Christianity opposed the ordination of women with vigour. The Roman Catholic and Orthodox churches still refuse even to discuss the possibility of women's ordination.

An obvious consequence of the churches' continuing failure to support gender equality – in practice if not in theory – is the alienation of women and men sympathetic to the ideal. This is not to say that huge numbers of women leave the churches in a conscious act of protest, but that one of the reasons that each successive generation since the 1960s has been less likely to attend than the one before may be that many women and men are no longer in sympathy with the churches' implicit or explicit messages about gender roles. Women who refuse to submit to male authority may struggle with a religion that has male clergy, a male God, and a male saviour; and women who want a career on equal terms with men may be alienated by churches that privilege women's domestic roles. They may abandon Christianity altogether, try to reform it, or find themselves attracted to the new holistic forms of spirituality that tend to be run by women for women and which offer direct benefit in terms of personal empowerment.

But this cannot be the whole story, for despite women's defection from the churches (the single most important direct cause of congregational decline), they continue to attend in larger numbers than men. For some, it would seem, the traditional attractions of Christianity remain, not least its ability to affirm women's domestic roles and offer support to family life. Large numbers of women continue to enjoy the satisfactions of an intense relationship with Jesus Christ. Others, particularly in some of the more liberal and mystical forms of Christianity, are experimenting with new forms of spirituality that require less by way of female submission. Some women have been admitted to positions of authority in the church, and a handful have even become bishops.

In the southern hemisphere the story is different again, for here the number of women in the churches is growing rather than declining, and women play a significant rule in Christianity's recent growth. Although a traditional message about male headship is more common than in the West, masculine authority is tempered in Charismatic Christianity by the presence of the Holy Spirit. Not only can the Spirit be represented in feminine terms as gentle, flowing, loving, and nurturing, it also offers direct empowerment to all who admit it into their lives, irrespective of their sex. Far from remaining external, commanding, and forbidding, God as Spirit enters into the most intimate relationship with the believer, empowering from within. Rather than imposing its will from above, the Spirit works through individual lives, bodies, and personalities, conferring authority as it does so. Lest the empowered overreach themselves, however, the Spirit is checked by the Word. That which is contrary to scripture – and thus to male headship – may be condemned as the work of evil spirits rather than the Spirit of God. Given lack of support for gender equality in many of the poorer countries of the world, this message supports a wider social consensus.

The success of Christianity across the centuries may lie, in part, in the delicate balance it has managed to maintain between male and female interests. While supporting the former, it has also made significant concessions to the latter. While affirming masculine domination, it has tempered and qualified it by emphasizing the importance of the gentler, more loving, more feminine virtues. While presenting a rhetoric of egalitarianism, it has ensured that male privilege has been firmly embedded in its own life. In this way it has been able to uphold patriarchal arrangements, whilst subjecting them to critique and control. Equally, it has managed to affirm women and appeal to them, without encouraging them to rebel against their masters. By appealing to greater numbers of women than to men, but in retaining and supporting male control, it may have achieved the best possible outcome in the male-dominated societies of which it has been an integral part.

The shift towards gender equality in modern Western societies poses a serious threat to traditional Christian imagery, teaching, and organization. For men, Christianity's role in reinforcing masculine domination becomes less relevant, whilst for women its usefulness as a way of gaining access to male power and subverting it from within becomes less important. As women as well as men come to place greater authority on the value of their own unique subjective-lives, they become more resistant to the ready-made roles into which the church would have them fit – however highly exalted. Outside the West, however, where full gender equality wins far less support, Christianity's delicate balancing act continues to prove effective. One might say that Christianity is most successful as a 'woman's religion' when it finds itself in a 'man's world' – a world it helps to reinforce, whilst ameliorating its excesses.

Chapter 13
Should AIDS be treated differently from other diseases?

The following text is extracted from *HIV/AIDS: A Very Short Introduction* by Alan Whiteside

Should AIDS be treated differently from other diseases? Should it be dealt with as a crisis or as a long-term development issue? This is an ongoing debate with no single or simple answer. Let me sum up the points I have made in this book.

AIDS is primarily a sexually transmitted infection affecting young adults. The spread is silent and the long incubation period means the virus has infected many people before illnesses manifest and the threat is apparent. Eminent British scientist Professor Roy Anderson modelled the course of the epidemic and estimated it will take 130 years to work through the global population.

There is no cure. There are treatments, but these remain relatively expensive. In poor countries, the cost of treating one AIDS patient is many times the average expenditure on health. Even if money were no object, there are human resource constraints to providing treatment. Science has made huge strides, but there will be no vaccine or microbicide available in the medium term.

AIDS is already having a devastating impact on some countries. In Swaziland, the chance of a 15-year-old boy living to 50 years is

28%, for a girl it is just 22%. Before AIDS, it was 92% and 97% respectively. The UNDP estimated 2004 life expectancy in Botswana to be 34.9 years. Populations in some African countries are projected to decline. Reversing life expectancies and falling populations are events unknown in the past 200 years. Economists question whether economic growth is possible in these circumstances; sociologists and political scientists have not begun to consider the ramifications.

The debate between normalization and exceptionalism is sterile. AIDS is exceptional and needs to be treated as such. But the measures needed to deal with the schisms and fractures that give rise to the epidemic are long term. Preventing AIDS means equitable development: providing education, health, employment opportunities, and social support. These are development goals, and not (just) about HIV/AIDS.

Perceptions

The innovative responses needed mean we must change perceptions. In spatial terms, the worst of the epidemic and hence its worst impacts are geographically bounded. Early fears that HIV would spread widely and uniformly were unfounded, and not all parts of the world are equally affected. Through a mixture of circumstance and predisposition, areas of Africa are particularly badly hit, though the smaller epidemics of Eastern Europe may have devastating consequences because of their demographic circumstances.

In temporal terms, AIDS shows how limited our time horizon is. Humanity has difficulty in taking long-term views. Most planning is geared to three to five year strategies. We want immediate solutions and to believe things will get better. Companies do not project declining profits; politicians do not warn of bleak futures. Humans see things in the short term and through rose-tinted glasses. But AIDS requires a long-term, realistic view. We know the number of illnesses and deaths will increase, in fact there is an awful predictability about HIV/AIDS and what it has the potential to do, and we need to get to grips with this.

Perhaps a key is to change our perspective. How would our great grandchildren see the epidemic if they were looking back from 2108? For them, HIV/AIDS will have been an historical event. If we develop this thinking, then history could provide ideas, paradigms, and methodologies for understanding and responding. There are lessons from the past we can apply; we need to learn from history and historians.

Prevention imperatives

Most important is avoiding future infections. AIDS is devastating for households, families, and society at large. Preventing infections means, in economic language, future costs will not have to be borne, additional human suffering will be averted. Prevention must remain the priority. If we knew what worked, it would be clear where resources should go, but as the book shows there are no easy answers. The drivers of the epidemic are multifaceted and responses need to take cognizance of the complexity of society, economies, and political management. We need to better understand sexuality.

There are effective targeted and technical interventions for early epidemics. This was seen in prevention of transmission through infected blood, responses to infection among drug users in Europe, and the timely interventions among sex workers in Thailand and Senegal. When the epidemic spreads beyond these populations, prevention becomes more haphazard and less successful.

There are three main lessons from the last 25 years. The first is that leadership is crucial. With strong, supportive leadership, prevention becomes possible; without it, it is extremely difficult. An editorial in *The Lancet* ahead of the 2004 International AIDS Conference in Bangkok identified the willingness of political leaders to acknowledge the crisis and implement interventions swiftly as the most important factor in changing the course of the epidemic. Uganda, Thailand, and Cambodia were singled out as countries where this happened.

The second area is gender and gender equity. Globally, HIV disproportionately infects and affects women. Not only are they more likely to be HIV positive, but they bear the burden of care and support. Prevention must empower women; give them choice over whom they have sex with, when, and how. Men must accept this and not feel threatened.

The final concerns around prevention messages are what they are and who is targeted. A narrow focus on abstinence and fidelity is unrealistic, hypocritical, and stigmatizing. The emphasis should be on responsible sexual behaviour rather than scare tactics. The discourse needs to move from sex to relationships, teaching people how to negotiate and develop responsible and loving interactions. Young people need to be inculcated with the behaviours and values that allow them to protect themselves from HIV and lead fulfilling lives. There is little point in targeting people whose sexual behaviours are set and unlikely to change. Single-component interventions do not work anywhere, and no general approach will work everywhere.

The treatment debate

When prevention fails, treatment is necessary. It is to the credit of science and activists that this is widely available and increasingly affordable. It took mobilization, militant campaigning, and legal action to bring the price of treatment within the means of poorer countries.

Treatment is still not universally accessible, nor will it be. With the current drugs and modes of administering them, there are simply not the human resources and infrastructure to provide treatment to all. For example, in 2004 Mozambique had under 800 doctors, a third of whom were foreign, fewer than 0.3 per 1,000 people. Providing ART to all who need it would need at least an additional 200 doctors plus nurses, pharmacists, and other staff. Health systems are under pressure, and staff are being diverted to AIDS.

Three key aspects of treatment are cost, sustainability, and access. The cheapest ART available is about US$ 150 per patient per year for the drugs alone. The associated testing, medical staff, and so on push the minimum cost to between US$ 200 and US$ 300. Put starkly, it costs between 0.54c and 0.82c a day to keep an infected person alive. One billion people, 19% of the world's population, live on less than a dollar a day, many in the countries worst affected by AIDS, such as Zambia, where 63% of people live on less than a dollar per day. Per capita government health expenditure, assessed in the 2006 World Health Report was US$ 3 in Nepal, US$ 6 in Nigeria, US$ 25 in Lesotho, and US$ 40 in Ukraine (in the UK, it is US$ 2,081 and the USA, US$ 2,548). In high-prevalence countries, the cost of therapy is many times the annual health budget. But it has also become apparent how complex providing ART is. There are reports of drugs being held back at ports because of unpaid duties, dispensaries running out of medicine, and people having to bribe their way into programmes.

Even with the limited treatment, there are questions of sustainability. Most treatment in the poor world is funded by donors, in particular the Global Fund and PEPFAR. At the end of March 2006, PEPFAR was supporting treatment for 561,000 men, women, and children. But PEPFAR was a five-year programme ending in 2008 with possible renewal to 2013, and the Global Fund projects too have a limited lifespan. The current challenge is to get people on treatment, but soon it will be to ensure there are the resources to continue, because patients need treatment for life.

Access is a complex issue, and choices have to be made. If not everyone can be treated, who do we treat? This debate creates huge difficulties among people working in the field of AIDS, human rights activists, and lawyers. Given that rationing is occurring, we need to ask on what basis should these decisions be made? In a seminal 2005 article in *PLoS Medicine* on rationing and its causes and consequences, Sydney Rosen and colleagues point out: 'As used by economists, rationing is a morally neutral concept. It does not imply an intent to deprive some people of a good, but rather describes the allocation of a resource of which there is not enough to go around.'

Should decisions be made on economic grounds, treating those who make the largest contribution to society first? There is a strong argument for giving health care workers preferential access – after all, they have to treat others. A WHO slogan is 'test, treat and retain'. Should treatment be made available on the basis of equity or gender? Or on the basis of some other criterion of what society wants and how it values people? There are no easy answers. Currently, decisions are made through a combination of medical imperatives, treating the sickest first; access, who can get to the treatment sites; and where the money is. Those with higher CD4 counts need the least clinical management. Using limited resources to manage crises is not optimal.

As the '3 by 5' initiative rolled out, it became apparent that providing treatment is not enough. The WHO recommended making antiretrovirals affordable and providing them free to the poor. What affordability means and who is poor are not defined. Our analysis shows that in low-income countries treatment should be free. Trying to implement user fees is a waste of scarce resources as they are costly to put in place and administer, and exemptions or waivers rarely reach those who need them. Asking the poor to pay for health care is not just impractical, it is also obscene. We looked at AIDS exceptionalism – should AIDS be treated free when other diseases are not? Other diseases are treated free where there is a public health reason to do so. Given the nature of the AIDS epidemic, providing free treatment should be an imperative even though the principle cannot be applied to all diseases or all in need.

Treatment issues also raise the question of targets. Should targets continue to be set given they won't be reached? Having a goal may be good from the perspective of a Western capitalist or activist, but some in the developing world view target-setting as a hypocritical activity because they are seldom met. This debate is broader than HIV/AIDS, it extends to the Millennium Development Goals, G8 commitments, and beyond.

Locating and dealing with impact

Much writing has described how people 'cope', but what is coping? For many it is simply struggling with increased impoverishment and misery. A household that does not access health care or child support but somehow continues to bring up its children can be said to be coping. But is this what society wants and will accept? Coping needs to be more than surviving.

The major impact is on human capital, which is increasingly recognized as critical for long-term development. It is being steadily and insidiously eroded. The illness and deaths of adults has effects across society. In government work gets done inefficiently, more slowly, or not at all. For the private sector, productivity is reduced and costs increased. Among farmers, it means there is less labour at critical times. The impact is intergenerational, as children with sick parents will not get the emotional and financial investment they need. Having a generation of orphans growing up uncared for and under-educated creates long-term problems. The long-wave complex impacts of HIV/AIDS are not appreciated.

Impact is gendered. Young women are afraid of dying and leaving their children, and they feel powerless to prevent infection. Older women, who bear the brunt of the social, care-taking, economic, and emotional burdens of the epidemic in their families, are supporting growing numbers on shrinking incomes.

Social transfers, sustainability, and the role of governments

In early 2006 at a Global Partners Forum on Children Affected by HIV and AIDS, British Deputy Minister for International Development, Gareth Thomas, identified social welfare as a core issue for debate. This means ensuring a minimum standard of living and access to essential services for all. The experience of rich countries has proven that social welfare is central to proper support for the most vulnerable, indeed free schooling and health facilities provide the basis for development. It is hypocritical to apply a different standard to poorer countries. Rather, we need to ensure social transfers, such as child benefits and social pensions, are the norm in all developing countries.

Dealing realistically with HIV prevention and AIDS does not lie only in responding to the disease but in addressing the underlying causes: poverty and inequality. This requires global reform in trade and international commitments. In the short term, social welfare programmes will go a long way to meeting the needs. But these interventions are not 'sustainable' as the word is currently used. Countries and communities won't graduate from needing support in the short or medium term, and questions of what 'sustainable development' actually is need to be posed.

Adam Smith argued centuries ago that governments should provide stability and law. In fact, we can and should demand far more of our governments at both the national and international levels. There are basic rights to health, education, incomes, and shelter. If these were met, we would not have the epidemic we currently face.

It bodes ill for humankind that we do not respond adequately to HIV/AIDS. We will face many other challenges. These include new, more easily spread diseases needing innovative, rapid public health responses. We confront global equity issues such as access to water. Climate change desperately requires international and coordinated action. AIDS is a harbinger, the first of many new and alarming challenges, and has given us the opportunity to learn. Only time will tell if we did.

Chapter 14
Are we becoming more intelligent?

The following text is extracted from *Intelligence: A Very Short Introduction* by Ian J. Deary

If my score on an IQ-type test is higher than yours, then does it mean that I am brighter/cleverer than you? If the test used was one of the best indicators of the general intelligence factor, or if it was one of the more comprehensive test batteries, such as one of the Wechsler tests, then we might be persuaded provisionally to accept that conclusion and ask for more information. We might be further persuaded if we were genetically related and lived in a similar culture. The next dataset calls the mental ability testing enterprise into question by demonstrating large differences in mental test scores *in just those situations where we might expect similarity*. The key researcher involved is James Flynn, a political scientist working at the University of Otago, New Zealand. He has provided researchers in the field of human intelligence with a scientific conundrum and massive communal headache.

The first thing Flynn brought to serious scientific scrutiny was that mental test companies had to renorm their scores every so often. This rather boring-sounding, technical problem was the source of one of the largest unexplained puzzles in the field of intelligence research today. When you buy a mental test from a psychometric company, you get the test questions and the answers, and you get instructions for giving the test in a standard way so that everyone who takes the test gets an equal chance to score well on it. But, imagine that you have now tested someone on the test: you will realize that you need something else. The person's score does not mean anything unless you have some indication of what is a bad, good, and indifferent score. Thus, with the test, when you buy it, you will get a booklet of normative scores, or 'norms'. This is a series of tables which indicate how any given score fits into the population's scores. Usually they are divided for age, because some test scores change with age. Therefore, you can find out how your testee did when compared with their age peers. Usually the tables with tell you what percentage of the population would have scored better and worse than the score that your testee obtained. Those of us with children and who measured their heights and compared them with the population average for their ages will be familiar with this type of referencing.

James Flynn noticed that these tables of norms had to be changed every several years. As new generations came along they were scoring too well on the tests. The tests seemed to be getting easier. A generation or two after the companies produced the tables of normative scores, the 'average' person of the later generation was scoring way above the 'average' person of the earlier generation. For example, 20-somethings tested in the 1980s were doing better on the same test than 20-somethings from the 1950s. The norms were becoming outdated – 'obsolete' was Flynn's term. (There's an ironic parallel with the trend in A-level results in England. Children have been scoring better than they used to on these tests, with resulting arguments about whether the teaching is better or the examinations are getting easier. At least, in the case of IQ-type tests, the content has remained the same.)

The response of the test companies was to 'renorm' the tests. The norms tables were altered so that, as time went on, it became harder to achieve a score that got you above any given percentage of your peers. Thus, if you scored *the exact same test score on the exact same test* in, say, 1950 and 1970, you would have a higher IQ in 1950 than in 1970. In fact, it can be seen as worse than that.

Let's say you take the test on the last day that the institution testing you used the old norms. You take the test and you obtain a given score. The tester looks up the norms tables and states that you make the cut above some percentage of your age peers. If you took the same test on the first day of the new norms the same score would put you significantly further down the percentage of the population. In fact, the test companies would not always alter the norms tables. The other manoeuvre they adopted was to make the test harder so that you had to take a new, harder test to get to the same point on the population scale.

In summary, as the 20th century progressed, the whole population's scores on some well-known mental tests were improving when compared with same-age people generations earlier. Just as average height has increased over generations, people began to wonder if intelligence was rising.

Flynn published a scientific paper in *Psychological Bulletin* in 1984 that gave IQ test-users an alarm call to a potential disaster. 'Everyone knew' that tests had to be renormed every so often, but Flynn quantified the effect and spelled out its consequences. He quantified the effect in a smart piece of psychological detective work. He searched for every study he could find in which groups of people were given two different IQ tests for which the norms were collected at least 6 years apart. This is the key idea. Flynn set about asking: what would the sample's estimated IQs be when compared with the earlier and the later norms? For clarity, he decided to look exclusively at samples of white Americans. He found 73 studies, involving a total of 7,500 people, aged from 2 to 48 years. These studies involved the Stanford-Binet and the Wechsler scales, tests at the very centre of the intelligence testing world.

Flynn found that subjects' estimated IQs were higher when they were compared with older norms, by contrast with more recent ones. On perusing all the samples involved, it became clear that the effect was fairly constant over the period from 1932 to 1978.

During that time white Americans gained over 0.3 of an IQ point every year, about 14 IQ points over the epoch. So, over the middle part of the 20th century, the American IQ rose by a massive amount. Flynn warned us:

> If two Stanford-Binet or Wechsler tests were normed at different times, the later test can easily be 5 or 10 points more difficult than the earlier, and any researcher who has assumed the tests were of equivalent difficulty will have gone astray. (p. 39)

> Allowing for obsolescence in intelligence testing is just as essential as allowing for inflation in economic analysis. (p. 44)

This takes some reckoning with and becomes even more surprising when the trend in SAT scores is added to the picture. The Scholastic Aptitude Test (SAT) is a high-level test taken at the end of school by America's educational elite. It is well documented that, over the period in which IQ scores were rising, the verbal scores – call it general knowledge for now – on the SAT were declining. And SAT scores and IQ scores are very highly correlated: yet one is decreasing over time while the other increases. If the IQ increases over time reflect a real rise in intelligence, and the SAT decreases are real decrements in knowledge, then one is forced to conclude that that aspect of the SAT that does not depend on intelligence (remember, IQ and SAT are highly correlated) must have gone down. Something that determines SAT scores (but not intelligence level) must have suffered massively at the same time that IQ went up. As Flynn worried:

> But it is precisely at this point that one's head begins to spin: do less demanding textbooks and low-level TV programs raise intelligence while lowering verbal skills; do declining standards in schools sharpen the mind while undermining study habits; does student absenteeism mean students are engaged in mentally demanding tasks while missing out on knowledge; does a demoralised family environment boost IQ while lowering motivation? (p. 38)

Perhaps, though, it's not as bad as that. It could just be that the test companies are not testing appropriately representative groups of people in their attempts at making up their norms. They might be going out generation after generation and getting it wrong by testing evermore biased, more clever samples for their norms tables, making it harder for those being tested to do well by comparison. Or perhaps the contents of the tests are steadily leaking out over time to the public so that people in successive generations have had more experience with the items? Thus, at the end of his first large-scale study, James Flynn came up with three points that might explain the 'massive gains' that successive American generations were attaining in IQ scores.

1. *Artefact.* The gains might be 'not real, but an artefact of sampling error'. That is, the groups recruited to provide norms might, over time, become more biased toward containing cleverer people. This is very unlikely to have occurred in such a systematic way as to make all later normative samples brighter than all earlier ones. But even if this is the explanation, it still makes scores across IQ tests non-comparable.

2. *Test sophistication.* Successive generations might not actually be more intelligent; they might just be scoring better on the tests for some reason that we have to go and find. This leaves us the large, additional problem of explaining the reason for SAT test scores declining.

3. *A real intelligence increase.* If the test score differences represent real increases in intelligence, they are very hard to explain. Flynn tried to examine the most likely candidate: that socio-economic improvements accounted for the IQ gains across generations. However, the gargantuan alterations that would be needed in living standards to account for the IQ changes were just not plausible.

James Flynn wanted more definitively to identify the source of the rising IQ scores. Broadening out from the USA, he sought examples of IQ test scores that had been collected across generations. Here's how he described that search:

> The method used to collect data can be simply put. Questionnaires, letters, or personal appeals (usually a combination of all three) were sent to all those researchers known to be interested in IQ trends on the basis of scholarly correspondence and the exchange of publications. One-hundred sixty-five scholars from 35 countries were contacted. They came from Europe (every nation except Albania, Denmark, Greece, and Portugal); Asia (Japan, India, and Israel); Latin America (Argentina, Brazil, Chile, Cuba, Mexico, and Venezuela); the Caribbean (Barbados and the U.S. Virgin Islands); and the Commonwealth (Australia, Canada, and New Zealand). American data were available from a previous study. Military authorities in charge of psychological testing were contacted in every European country, plus Australia, Canada, Greenland, Iceland, and New Zealand, as were 21 educational research institutes in Western Europe and the Commonwealth. (p. 171)

Key dataset 11

This is typical of James Flynn. He does nothing by halves, and he has thrown over 20 years of his academic life into scouring the world for data to address the 'rising IQ' problem. Some of Flynn's strongest data came from military samples, in those countries where nearly all young men were given IQ tests at entry to compulsory military service. Figure 2 illustrates some of Flynn's data.

Here's how to look at Figure 2. The vertical scale at the left-hand side is an IQ scale. Along the horizontal are some different countries from which Flynn got good data. In each country the most recently available data have been set at an arbitrary IQ score of 100. These appear at the top of the 5 vertical lines. An IQ of 100 is, by an arbitrary definition, the population average. For each of the 5 countries in the Figure there were earlier testings of the

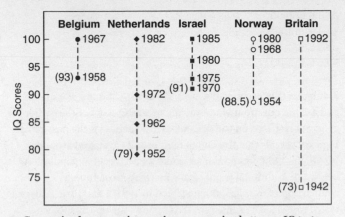

2. Generation by generation, nations are scoring better on IQ tests

same population. The dates down the dotted vertical lines shows just how much lower the populations' IQs were in earlier testings. Note the dots on each vertical line with a date against them: these dates are when the IQ testings of the population took place. If you read across from these dots/dates to the left you can see what the average IQ of the population was at that date, compared with the 100 score of the most recently tested population. Please note that we should expect that all of these testings would give rise to average IQs of 100. They do not. Whenever a population was tested at an earlier date the imputed IQ average was lower. The effect found among American whites was also found in many other countries, leading Flynn to name his 1987 *Psychological Bulletin* article 'Massive IQ gains in 14 nations'.

Take the example of the Netherlands. Since 1945 the Dutch military have tested almost all young men in the Netherlands on 40 of the 60 items of Raven's Progressive Matrices. This is a non-verbal mental ability test and is supposed to be quite good at testing general intelligence. Flynn examined these data and reported the percentage of young men who were scoring more than 24 of the 40 items correct. The percentages were:

31.2% in 1952
46.4% in 1962
63.2% in 1972
82.2% in 1981/2.

Setting the 1982 scores to a mean IQ of 100, one can work back
and ask the question: what was the mean IQ score of the earlier
generations based on the percentage that achieved the pass rates?
Figure 2 reveals that the Dutch men in 1972 averaged around
IQ 90, the 1962 population around 85, and the 1952 population
below 80. Additional proof of this increase arose from a
comparison of over 2,800 men tested in 1981/2 and their fathers
tested in 1954. The sons were 18 IQ points higher than their
fathers who had been tested $27\frac{1}{2}$ years earlier. Thus, we see this
puzzling effect in people who are genetically related and who have
lived in the same culture, where we would expect similar average
IQ scores.

Look again at Figure 2. Norwegian data for approximately the
same period show gains for later generations too, but they are
smaller than those of the Dutch. Belgian military data showed a
rise of 7 IQ points over the relatively short period from 1958 to
1967. New Zealand children gained an average of 7.7 IQ points
between 1936 and 1968 (data not shown). Two further sets of data
from Flynn's large number of comparisons are shown: Israelis
gained 11 IQ points over the 15 years from 1970 to 1985 and people
in the United Kingdom went from a putative mean IQ of 73 in
1942 to 100 in 1992.

This last increase makes a good illustration of the impact if these
changes were real alterations in intelligence levels. Compared with
a mean of 100 in 1992, the mean for the population in 1942 would
be almost at a level that indicated mental handicap for the *average*
person. (It is this consideration that makes me very sceptical
about the veracity of these supposed 'IQ gains'.) In the end, Flynn
found reasonable data on 14 nations and for a generation

(30 years) he found IQ gains between 5 and 25 points, with an average of 15. These data are stunning, and very challenging for researchers in the field of intelligence.

One key fact to focus on when thinking about the 'Flynn effect' of rising IQ scores is that the biggest effects tend to occur in so-called culturally reduced tests. That is, the rises occur most markedly in those tests that do not seem to have contents that can easily be learned. For example, Raven's Progressive Matrices is among the tests that show the highest gains. Yet Raven's Matrices involves finding the correct answer that completes an abstract pattern. It has no words, no numbers, nothing really that can be taught so that the later generation will do better than the former. Flynn's review of his massive datasets confirmed this.

> A consensus about the significance of generational IQ gains depends, therefore, on whether they manifest themselves on culturally reduced tests like the Raven's. These tests maximise problem-solving and minimise the need for more specific skills and familiarity with words and symbols. [There are] strong data for massive gains on culturally reduced tests: Belgium, the Netherlands, Norway, and Edmonton show gains ranging from 7 to 20 points over periods from 9 to 30 years; when the rates of gain are multiplied by 30 years, they suggest that the current generation has gained 12–24 points on this kind of test. Tentative data from other nations are in full agreement. This settles the question at issue: IQ gains since 1950 reflect a massive increase in problem-solving ability and not merely an increased body of learned content. (p. 185)

The Flynn effect is well established. Its importance is reflected in the eponymous title, and in the interest it has attracted since the late 1980s. The American Psychological Association had a full meeting on the issue, and published a book in which many experts sought an answer to it. It is easy, and accurate, to summarize by saying that experts are dumbfounded. There are two broad responses to the Flynn effect.

The first response is to suggest that the Flynn effect is real, marking an actual improvement in brain power in successive generations across this century. People who opt for this account suggest that we have a good exemplar in height. Human height has increased across the century as a result of better nutrition and general health, so why not intelligence? Flynn himself seemed not to favour this option. He worked out that, in countries such as the Netherlands and France, where there have been high IQ gains across generations, teachers should now be faced with classes in which 25% are gifted and where geniuses have increased 60-fold! 'The result should be a cultural renaissance too great to be overlooked.' (p. 187) Flynn searched French and Dutch newspapers, especially periodicals relating to education, from the late 1960s to the present and found no mention of any great increase in intellectual achievements by newer generations.

The second response suggests that the Flynn effect is an artefact. It is not the case that people are more intelligent. Instead, what has happened is that people have become more familiar with the test materials. Children's toys, magazines, television programmes, computer games, and so forth might contain materials that have IQ-item-like properties, and so people do better on the tests when they come across them. This might be termed the 'Early Learning Centre' theory.

There is one thing to note about the Flynn effect that Flynn himself has been keen to emphasize. Though the effect is clearly important, it does not compromise the validity of mental test scores *within* generations. Mental test scores, despite the 'massive gains' through time, do retain their reliability, their ability to predict educational and job successes, and their heritability, but only *within* each generation. The key point is that something in the environment (many researchers believe that it has to be the environment because some of the across-generation samples tested fathers and sons) of many countries across the middle years of the 20th century has led to ability scores increasing substantially.

Flynn makes a telling point when he asks us to reflect on the fact that being born a generation or so apart can make a difference of 15 IQ points. We have no good account of the causes for this change; it is officially mysterious. Given, though, that he could find no evidence for the present generation's genius in achievement over former generations, Flynn says that IQ tests like Raven's do not measure intelligence, but only some correlate of intelligence, which he calls 'abstract problem-solving ability'. Further, he insists that differences in this ability are 15 points between successive generations, and these differences must arise from some environmental factor. He concludes that IQ test differences cannot be used to make trustworthy comparisons of the intelligence of different generations or of different cultural groups.

The reader might like to reflect on the Flynn effect and its causes, not least because some fresh thinking on this matter might offer psychologists a foothold on a slippery problem. If there was a prize to be offered in the field of human intelligence research, it would be for the person who can explain the 'Flynn effect' of the 'rising IQ'.

Chapter 15
How will the world end?

The following text is extracted from *Global Catastrophes: A Very Short Introduction* by Bill McGuire

We could face oblivion tomorrow or have to wait 100,000 or more years before a city is obliterated or a thousand millennia before the world plunges into cosmic winter beneath a cloud of pulverized rock. But whenever the skies next fall, how will it affect us? This will depend upon three things: (i) the size of the object, (ii) how quickly it is travelling, and (iii) whether it hits the land or the ocean. Everything else being equal, the larger the impactor the more devastating and widespread will be its effects. A body in the 50–100-metre size range carries enough destructive power to wipe out a major city or a small European country or US state. The level and extent of associated devastation will increase progressively with larger impactors until the critical 2-kilometre size is reached. In addition to causing appalling destruction on a regional or sub-continental scale, the arrival of an object of this size will affect the entire planet through engendering a period of dramatic cooling and reduced plant growth. For impactors larger than 2 kilometres the effects on the planet's ecosystems become progressively more severe until mass extinctions wipe out a significant percentage of all species. The 10-kilometre object that struck the Earth off the Mexican coast at the end of the Cretaceous period, 65 million years ago, not only finished off the dinosaurs but also two-thirds of all species living at the time. Even more disturbingly, there is evidence of a major impact event at the end of the Permian period some 250 million years ago that left fewer than 10 per cent of species alive. In all, at least 7 out of 25 major extinctions in the geological record have been linked with evidence for large impacts, although there is a school of thought that plays down the environmental effects of impact events and prefers to implicate huge outpourings of basalt lava in the great extinctions of the past.

The destructive potential of a chunk of rock hurtling into the Earth is directly related to the kinetic energy it carries, and this reflects not only the size of the object but also the velocity of the collision. Because they travel substantially faster, therefore, impacts by so-called *long-period* comets, whose orbits carry them far out into interstellar space, cause more destruction than either NEAs or local comets that follow orbits confined to the heart of the solar system. Both the nature and scale of devastation also depend upon whether the impactor hits the land or the sea. Two-thirds of our planet's surface is covered by water, so statistically this is where the majority of asteroids and comets strike. In such cases, the amount of pulverized rock hurled into the atmosphere might be reduced, compared to a land collision. However, this small benefit is likely to be at least partly countered by the formation of giant tsunamis capable of wreaking havoc across an entire ocean basin. Furthermore, the gigantic quantities of water and salt injected into the atmosphere may severely affect the climate and even temporarily wipe out our protective ozone shield. Most of the evidence for the environmental effects of impacts comes from studies of just two events, one small and the other enormous.

At the low end of the scale, in 1908 a small asteroid, estimated at around 50 metres across, penetrated the Earth's atmosphere and exploded less than 10 kilometres above the surface of Siberia in a region known as Tunguska. This huge blast, which expended roughly the energy equivalent of 800 Hiroshima atomic bombs, was heard over an area four times the size of the UK and flattened over 2,000 square kilometres of full-grown forest. The blast registered on seismographs thousands of kilometres distant and the atmospheric shock wave was picked up by barographs time and again as it travelled three times around the planet before dissipating. The gas and dust generated by the explosion led to exceptionally bright night skies over Europe, sufficient – according to one contemporary report – to allow cricket to be played in London after midnight. Because of its inaccessibility, the first Russian expedition did not reach Tunguska until a quarter of a century later, when Leonid Kulik and his team were perplexed by the absence of the huge crater they were expecting. Instead they found a circular patch of badly charred and flattened trees 60 kilometres across, formed by the airburst as the rock disintegrated explosively due to the huge stresses caused by entry into the atmosphere. As the region was sparsely inhabited, casualties due to the impact were small, with perhaps a few killed and up to 20 injured, although reports are understandably sketchy. Four hours later, however, and the Earth would have rotated sufficiently to bring the great city of St Petersburg into the asteroid's range and the result would have been catastrophic.

The Tunguska event pales into insignificance when compared to what happened off the coast of Mexico's Yucatan Peninsula 65 million years earlier. Here a 10-kilometre asteroid or comet – its exact nature is uncertain – crashed into the sea and changed our world forever. Within microseconds, an unimaginable explosion released as much energy as billions of Hiroshima bombs detonated simultaneously, creating a titanic fireball hotter than the Sun that vaporized the ocean and excavated a crater 180 kilometres across in the crust beneath. Shock waves blasted upwards, tearing the atmosphere apart and expelling over a hundred trillion tonnes of molten rock into space, later to fall across the globe. Almost immediately an area bigger than Europe would have been flattened and scoured of virtually all life, while massive earthquakes rocked the planet. The atmosphere would have howled and screamed as *hypercanes* five times more powerful than the strongest hurricane ripped the landscape apart, joining forces with huge tsunamis to batter coastlines many thousands of kilometres distant.

Even worse was to follow. As the rock blasted into space began to rain down across the entire planet, so the heat generated by its re-entry into the atmosphere irradiated the surface, roasting animals alive as effectively as an oven grill, and starting great conflagrations that laid waste the world's forests and grasslands and turned fully a quarter of all living material to ashes. Even once the atmosphere and oceans had settled down, the crust had stopped shuddering, and the bombardment of debris from space had ceased, more was to come. In the following weeks, smoke and dust in the atmosphere blotted out the Sun and brought temperatures plunging by as much as 15 degrees Celsius. In the growing gloom and bitter cold the surviving plant life wilted and died while those herbivorous dinosaurs that remained slowly starved. Life in the oceans fared little better as poisons from the global wildfires and acid rain from the huge quantities of sulphur injected into the atmosphere from rocks at the site of the impact poured into the oceans, wiping out three-quarters of all marine life. After years of freezing conditions the gloom following the so-called Chicxulub impact would eventually have lifted, only to reveal a terrible Sun blazing through the tatters of an ozone layer torn apart by the chemical action of nitrous oxides concocted in the impact fireball: an *ultraviolet spring* – hard on the heels of the cosmic winter – that fried many of the remaining species struggling precariously to hang on to life. So enormously was the natural balance of the Earth upset that according to some it might have taken hundreds of thousands of years for the post-Chicxulub Earth to return to what passes for normal. When it did the age of the great reptiles was finally over, leaving the field to the primitive mammals – our distant ancestors – and opening an evolutionary trail that culminated in the rise and rise of the human race. But could we go the same way? To assess the chances, let me look a little more closely at the destructive power of an impact event.

At Tunguska, destruction of the forests resulted partly from the great heat generated by the explosion, but mainly from the blast wave that literally pushed the trees over and flattened them against the ground. The strength of this blast wave depends upon what is called the *peak overpressure*, that is the difference between ambient pressure and the pressure of the blast wave. In order to cause severe destruction this needs to exceed 4 pounds per square inch, an overpressure that results in wind speeds that are over twice the force of those found in a typical hurricane. Even though tiny compared with, say, the land area of London, the enormous overpressures generated by a 50-metre object exploding low overhead would cause damage comparable with the detonation of a very large nuclear device, obliterating almost everything within the city's orbital motorway. Increase the size of the impactor and things get very much worse. An asteroid just 250 metres across would be sufficiently massive to penetrate the atmosphere; blasting a crater 5 kilometres across and devastating an area of around 10,000 square kilometres – that is about the size of the English county of Kent. Raise the size of the asteroid again, to 650 metres, and the area of devastation increases to 100,000 square kilometres – about the size of the US state of South Carolina.

Terrible as this all sounds, however, even this would be insufficient to affect the entire planet. In order to do this, an impactor has to be at least 1.5 kilometres across, if it is one of the speedier comets, or 2 kilometres in diameter if it is one of the slower asteroids. A collision with one of these objects would generate a blast equivalent to 100,000 *million* tonnes of TNT, which would obliterate an area 500 kilometres across – say the size of England – and immediately kill perhaps tens of millions of people, depending upon the location of the impact.

The real problems for the rest of the world would start soon after as dust in the atmosphere began to darken the skies and reduce the level of sunlight reaching the Earth's surface. By comparison with the huge Chicxulub impact it is certain that this would result in a dramatic lowering of global temperatures but there is no consensus on just how bad this would be. The chances are, however, that an impact of this size would result in appalling weather conditions and crop failures at least as severe as those of the 'Year Without a Summer', which followed the 1815 eruption of Indonesia's Tambora volcano. As mentioned in the last chapter, with even developed countries holding sufficient food to feed their populations for only a month or so, large-scale crop failures across the planet would undoubtedly have serious implications. Rationing, at the very least, is likely to be the result, with a worst case scenario seeing widespread disruption of the social and economic fabric of developed nations. In the developing world, where subsistence farming remains very much the norm, widespread failure of the harvests could be expected to translate rapidly into famine on a biblical scale. Some researchers forecast that as many as a quarter of the world's population could succumb to a deteriorating climate following an impact of a 2-kilometre object. Anything much bigger and photosynthesis stops completely. Once this happens the issue is not how many people will die but whether the human race will survive. One estimate proposes that the impact of an object just 4 kilometres across will inject sufficient quantities of dust and debris into the atmosphere to reduce light levels below those required for photosynthesis.

Because we still don't know how many threatening objects there are out there nor whether they come in bursts, it is almost impossible to say when the Earth will be struck by an asteroid or comet that will bring to an end the world as we know it. Impact events on the scale of the Chicxulub dinosaur-killer only happen every several tens of millions of years, so in any single year the chances of such an impact are tiny. Any optimism is, however, tempered by the fact that – should the Shiva hypothesis be true – the next swarm of Oort Cloud comets could even now be speeding

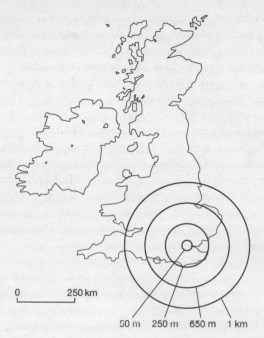

3. Predicted zones of total destruction for variously sized impacts centred on London

towards the inner solar system. Failing this, we may have only another thousand years to wait until the return of the dense part of the Taurid Complex and another asteroidal assault. Even if it turns out that there is no coherence in the timing of impact events, there is statistically no reason why we cannot be hit next year by an undiscovered NEA or by a long-period comet that has never before visited the inner solar system. Small impactors on the Tunguska scale pose less of a threat because their destructive footprints are tiny compared to the surface area of the Earth. It would be very bad luck if one of these struck an urban area, and most will fall in the sea. Although this might seem a good thing, a larger object striking the ocean would be very bad news indeed.

A 500-metre rock landing in the Pacific Basin, for example, would generate gigantic tsunamis that would cause massive damage to every coastal city in the hemisphere within 20 hours or so. The chances of this happening are actually quite high – about 1 per cent in the next 100 years – and the death toll could be in the tens of millions if not higher.

The most recent estimate of the frequency of 1-kilometre impacts is 600,000 years, but the youngest impact crater produced by an object of this size is almost a million years old. Of course, there could have been several large impacts since, which either occurred in the sea or have not yet been located on land. Fair enough, you might say, the threat is clearly out there, but is there anything on the horizon? Actually, there is. A dozen or so asteroids – mostly quite small – could feasibly collide with the Earth before 2100. Realistically, however, this is not very likely as the probabilities involved are not much greater than 1 in 10,000 – although bear in mind that these are pretty good odds. If this was the probability of winning the lottery then my local agent would be getting considerably more of my business. Most worrying is the 320-metre Near Earth Asteroid, MN4, discovered late in 2004 and recently named *Apophis*, the Greek name for the Egyptian God *Apep* – the destroyer. At one point, the probability of Apophis striking the Earth on 13 April 2029 was thought to be as high as 1 in 37. Now, to everyone's relief, those odds have increased to 1 in 8,000. Again, these may sound very long odds, but they are actually only 80 times greater than those offered during summer 2001 for England beating Germany 5–1 at football. A few years ago, scientists came up with an index – known as the Torino Scale – to measure the impact threat, and so far Apophis is the first object to register and sustain a value greater than zero. At present it scores a 1 on the scale – defined as 'an event meriting careful monitoring'. The object is the focus of considerable attention as efforts continue to better constrain its orbit, and it is perfectly possible – as we find out more – that it could rise to 1 on the Torino Scale, becoming an 'event meriting concern'. It is very unlikely, however, to go any higher, and let's hope that many years elapse before we encounter the first category 10 event – defined as 'a certain collision with global consequences'. Given sufficient warning we might be able to nudge an asteroid out of the Earth's way but due to its size, high velocity, and sudden appearance, we could do little about a new comet heading in our direction.